A Hungry
Mì Hungry

A Hungry Mi' Hungry

Traditional Jamaican Recipes & More . . . .

Rita Johnson

A HUNGRY MI HUNGRY

iUniverse books may be ordered through booksellers or by contacting:

iUniverse
1663 Liberty Drive
Bloomington, IN 47403
www.iuniverse.com
1-800-Authors (1-800-288-4677)

Because of the dynamic nature of the Internet, any web addresses or links contained in this book may have changed since publication and may no longer be valid. The views expressed in this work are solely those of the author and do not necessarily reflect the views of the publisher, and the publisher hereby disclaims any responsibility for them.

Any people depicted in stock imagery provided by Thinkstock are models, and such images are being used for illustrative purposes only. Certain stock imagery © Thinkstock.

ISBN: 978-1-4917-9983-3 (sc)
ISBN: 978-1-5320-0429-2 (hc)
ISBN: 978-1-5320-0197-0 (e)

Library of Congress Control Number: 2016910819

Print information available on the last page.

iUniverse rev. date: 07/30/2016

Dedication

This book is dedicated to my mother, the Jamaican queen of our family, E. A. Hislop. I am grateful to you for the love you have bestowed on us and the wonderful meals you provided for us when you were here. Now I am able to put these authentic recipes in this book. May God's blessing continue to be with you. You were and always will be, a wonderful mother who placed the needs of your children before your own. You were always there with a listening ear and a kind word when we needed it the most. You were our treasure and we all miss you very much; life has not been the same without you. My beautiful Jamaican queen you are extremely missed. I pray that this book will honor you.

Thank you Mama! I love you.

And to my children, for their inspiration and effort towards bringing this book to fruition.

Contents

Porridges

Sauces & Seasonings Plus . . .

Soups

Breads

Desserts

Drinks

Teas

Foreword

Writing this book gave me an opportunity to share my passion for meal preparation and taste that pierces the souls of all who partake. Over my years on this earth I have learned that while the eyes are the window to the soul, a succulent meal is the current that energizes the body that houses the soul.

It is my absolute pleasure to share these recipes with all my friends who love to cook, eat and enjoy their families. In each meal you will notice the difference between my cookbook and other cookbooks, in that the meals are made with organic seasonings, the desserts are made with no imitation flavoring; therefore, every bite will leave you savoring the taste. My favorites are highlighted with pictures; however, each meal promises a wonderful conversation and an evening, day, or morning of reminiscence.

The art of making a tasty meal is a talent based in creativity that I attribute to my creator God. Like most I feel compel to share my talents with all who are interested. Ten percent of the proceeds of this book will be donated to St. Jude.

It is an honor and a privilege to be a part of your conversation.

God's blessings and good meal!

Brief History on Jamaican Foods

The rich Jamaican cuisine is an exquisite blend of all the people who have inhabited the Island. The Jamaican motto "Out of Many One People" speaks to the culture of the Island, not only in terms of ethnicity, but also to the rich assortment of foods.

The history and foods of the Island started with the Arawak Indians (the original inhabitants of the Island), who were invaded by the Spanish. Their time under Spanish rule was short lived as the Spanish lost the Island to the British.

Under British rule slavery was introduced to the Island bringing people from the Gold Coast of Africa. When slavery ended, Indians, Chinese, Portuguese, and people from a few Middle Eastern countries came to the Island as indentured servants, further adding to the melting pot feel of the Island.

There are a lot of recipes, herbs, and spices that were generated by the Arawak Indians (bammy, corn, sweet potatoes, callaloo, beans, guavas, pineapples, papayas), the Spanish (escovitch fish, peas, and beans dishes, cattle, pigs, goats, and lard from animal fat, Seville and Valencia oranges, lime, lemon, tamarind, ginger, pomegranate, plantain, coconuts, grapes, figs, bananas, and sugar cane), the Maroons (various herbs and recipes), the Indians (spices – particularly curry), the Cantonese/Hakka (our world famous beef patties), the British (Jamaican fruit cake, corned beef, salt beef, Easter bun, tarts, pies, jams, and puddings), Jews, Chinese (pok choy and other vegetables), Scottish (porridge), and Africans (duckunoo, rundown).

All these different people brought with them, the attitude, the various spices, foods, and recipes from their homeland that have merged into this wonderful array of spicy, delectable delights that excite the palates of people around the globe.

In putting together this book of traditional Jamaican recipes, I hope to share the love of the Jamaican people and the enjoyment of the foods from my beautiful Island home. It is my wish that the meals from these recipes will bring your family together as it has done for mine over the years.

Besides the traditional Jamaican recipes, I have also included some of my favorite desserts. Enjoy!

Main Dishes

Cocktail Beef Patties

Pastry Dough

Ingredients:

4 cups all-purpose flour

1 teaspoon salt

3 teaspoons curry powder

1⅓ cup cold vegetable shortening

1 cup ice cold water (more if needed)

In a large bowl combine flour, salt and curry powder, mix together, then, cut small pieces of shortening into flour mixture: add ½ cup ice water and mix with your fingers until dough is formed, keep adding ice water 2-3 tablespoons at a time, until the dough is completed. Cut the dough into 2 large pieces. Wrap the dough in plastic wrap and refrigerate for at least 30 minutes.

Filling

Ingredients:

2 pounds ground beef

½ teaspoon seasoning salt (or to taste)

½ teaspoon black pepper

2 tablespoons soy sauce

1 teaspoon fresh thyme

2 teaspoons minced garlic

2 tablespoons vegetable or coconut oil

1 teaspoon Italian seasoning

2 teaspoons Scotch bonnet hot pepper sauce

½ cup scallions (minced green onions)

¼ cup seasoned breadcrumbs

1 teaspoon ground allspice

1 cup diced onions,

1-2 packs readymade pastry dough (if unable to make dough)

2 cups water

2 teaspoons curry powder

In a large bowl, place ground beef sprinkle with allspice and black pepper. Mix together and set aside. In large skillet heat oil, add onions, and sauté, then, add garlic, thyme, hot pepper sauce, curry powder and salt. Next, add ground beef, soy sauce, and Italian seasoning, mix together until meat is no longer pink, then, add water and continue stirring. Bring to a boil and add breadcrumbs and scallion, reduce heat and simmer for 2 minutes, let cool completely. Next, flour the surface and rolling pin, then, take 1 piece of the dough place it on the floured surface and roll into a circle. Use a bowl to make circles on the dough, then, cut around the circles. Next, place 2 very generous tablespoons of the filling into a half of the circle; next, moist the edges of the pastry with water. Fold the other half of the pastry over to seal, then, use a fork to crimp the edges, cut off any excess dough to make it neat. Repeat the process until the pastry dough and filling is finished. Next, line a baking sheet with parchment paper. Place the patties on prepared baking sheet. Preheat oven at 350°. Then brush the patties with egg wash and put in the oven. Bake until the patties are golden brown. Serve hot.

Beef Pot Roast

Ingredients:

1 3-4 pounds roast

1 small onion (diced)

½ teaspoon thyme

4 teaspoons teriyaki sauce

½ teaspoon seasoning salt

1 teaspoon Italian seasoning

½ teaspoon black pepper

3 cloves garlic (minced)

3 tablespoons marinade

½ teaspoon ground cloves

1 teaspoon steak seasoning

In large mixing bowl combine all seasoning, place pot roast in bowl and rub seasoning all over roast; refrigerate for about 8–12 hours turning occasionally so that seasoning is evenly distributed. Heat oven at 350° place roast in roasting pan without the seasoning, roast for 30 minutes turning a few times, add seasoning and then cover with foil paper; continue roasting for another 20 minutes or until cook to specification. Remove from oven let sit for at least 10 minutes before slicing.

Beef Meatloaf

Ingredients:

2 pounds ground beef

1 small onion (diced)

3 cloves garlic (minced)

½ medium green pepper, (diced)

1 teaspoon ground cloves

½ teaspoon black pepper

½ teaspoon Scotch bonnet hot pepper sauce

3 tablespoons Kikkoman teriyaki sauce

2 tablespoon Lawry's teriyaki sauce

½ teaspoon nutmeg

1 teaspoon seasoning salt

¼ cup ketchup + 3 tablespoons

1 egg beaten

¼ cup breadcrumbs

1 teaspoon Italian seasoning

1 teaspoon paprika

In large mixing bowl, combine ground beef and all seasonings except 3 tablespoons ketchup. Mix together with your fingers. In ungreased loaf tin place seasoned meat, flatten to form a loaf (even the top). Bake for 30 minutes at 375° then use pastry brush, to brush 3 tablespoons ketchup on the top. Reduce heat to 350° and bake for another 30 minutes. Slice and serve with mashed potatoes.

Gravy

Ingredients:

1 tablespoon margarine

Dash of black pepper

Dash of salt

¼ teaspoon Italian seasoning

1 teaspoon paprika

2 tablespoons ketchup

2 tablespoon minced onion

In small saucepan heat margarine, add all ingredients and water to saucepan stirring vigorously for about 2 minutes. Remove from heat and serve with meat loaf.

Easy Meat Loaf

Ingredients:

1½ pounds ground beef

2 eggs (beaten)

¾ cup milk

½ cup bread crumbs

¼ cup finely chopped bread onion

2 tablespoons freshly chopped parsley

1 teaspoon salt

¼ teaspoon black pepper

½ teaspoon ground sage

¼ cup ketchup

2 tablespoons brown sugar

1 teaspoon dry mustard

In a medium bowl, combine milk, eggs, bread crumbs, onion, parsley, salt, sage, and pepper. Add ground beef and mix well. Pour into ungreased loaf pan pat to form a loaf. Bake at 350° for 50 minutes. Drain the fat off, mix ketchup, brown sugar and mustard, spread over the top of the meat loaf and bake for additional 10 minutes. Serve hot.

Corned Beef and Cabbage

Ingredients:

1 can corn beef

1 small cabbage

1 small tomato (diced)

1 small onion (diced)

½ teaspoon black pepper

¼ teaspoon Mrs. Dash seasoning

1 tablespoon margarine

1 tablespoon olive oil

Cut cabbage in two then slice each piece in strips. Place in medium skillet and add onion, tomato, black pepper, Mrs. Dash seasoning, margarine and olive oil. Then cover and steam for about 3 minutes, stirring regularly. Remove from heat, open corn beef and cut in small squares, add corned beef to cabbage and stir. Cover and steam for 2 minutes. Serve hot with white rice.

Spicy Beef Stew

Ingredients:

2 pounds beef cubes

2 medium carrots (diced)

1 small onion (diced)

1 small potato (diced)

1 small sweet potato (cubed)

½ teaspoon seasoning salt

2 tablespoons soy sauce

2 tablespoons Lawry's Hawaii sauce

¼ teaspoon black pepper

¼ cup frozen green peas

2 sprigs thyme

1 bay leaf

½ teaspoon hot pepper sauce

1 teaspoon Italian seasoning

1 tablespoon margarine

6-8 cups water

½ teaspoon ground cloves

2 tablespoons vegetable or coconut oil

1 teaspoon Scotch bonnet hot pepper sauce

In mixing bowl combine beef and all seasoning except green peas. Rub together with fingers, cover and let sit for at least 2 hours. Place saucepan on medium heat, add vegetable oil, seasoned beef with all ingredients including green peas

Stir, together can also be done in slow cooker. Cover and cook until beef is tender. Simmer until gravy is thick. Serve with white rice.

Liver and Onions

Ingredients:

1 pack liver already sliced

1 medium onion cut in rings

3 cloves garlic diced

½ teaspoon seasoning salt

½ teaspoon black pepper

1 tablespoon soy sauce

2 tablespoons vegetable oil or coconut oil

Dash of scotch bonnet hot pepper sauce (optional)

Cut each piece of liver in two and put in a bowl. Pour all ingredients except oil on top and rub together with fingers. Let it sit for 10 minutes then heat oil over. medium heat and add the liver (one piece at a time). Allow it to brown on both sides then, add the seasoning from the bowl then cover and reduce the heat. Cook for 2 minutes. Gravy must be rich if needed add 1 tablespoon water to make enough gravy. Serve with white rice.

Stewed Peas

Ingredients:

1 Pack pinto beans or red peas

1 pound beef (cubed)

1 teaspoon seasoning salt (or as needed)

½ teaspoon black pepper

1 teaspoon Italian seasoning

2 medium carrots (diced)

2 sprigs thyme

½ small onion (diced)

2 stalks scallion/green onions (cut in small pieces)

2 cloves garlic minced

¼ cup flour

1 tin coconut milk

2 bay leaves

¼ teaspoon hot pepper sauce

¼ teaspoon ground pimento Wash peas and place in medium saucepan or slow cooker, ⅔ full of water. Next, add salt and leave to soak overnight so that peas can be easily cooked. On medium heat, cook peas and meat. When peas are cooked and meat is tender, add all other ingredients then use ¼ cup of flour to make little dumplings. Add coconut milk and taste to make sure it is to taste. Cover and cook until it is a semi thick consistency. Serve with white rice.

Tender Pepper steak

Ingredients:

1 pack steak (about 4 small steaks)

1 teaspoon steak seasoning

1 teaspoon Italian seasoning

2 tablespoons Kikkoman sauce

¼ teaspoon Scotch bonnet hot pepper sauce

½ teaspoon seasoned pepper

1 tablespoon teriyaki sauce

1 small onion (cut in rings)

1 small tomato diced

1 medium green bell pepper (cut in cubes)

In medium bowl season steak with all ingredients and set aside for at least 60 minutes. Preheat oven at 350°. Place steaks with all ingredients in a square baking dish, cover with foil paper and cook until tender. Gravy should be dark and rich. Serve hot.

Oxtail with Butter Beans

Ingredients:

3-4 pounds oxtail

2 sprigs thyme

1 can butter beans

¼ teaspoon black pepper

1 small onion (diced)

¼ teaspoon ground pimento

3 tablespoons soy sauce

¼ teaspoon seasoning salt

5 cups water

1 medium carrot (diced)

1 tablespoon teriyaki sauce

Dash of scotch bonnet hot pepper sauce

½ teaspoon ground cloves

Mix all seasoning together in large mixing bowl, then add oxtail and rub together with fingers let marinade over night. In pressure cooker pour water and seasoned oxtail, cover and pressure for about 7-10 minutes turn stove off and allow pressure cooker to cool then check the tenderness of the meat and cover with foil paper or other covers continue cooking until tender (can also be done in slow cooker). Taste to make sure seasoning is enough. Add butter beans to oxtail and cook for another 2 minutes to heat the beans. Serve with white rice or rice and peas.

Stewed Cow Foot

Ingredients:

2 pounds cow's foot

1 medium onion (diced)

½ teaspoon black pepper

1 teaspoon salt (or to taste)

¾ teaspoon Scotch bonnet hot pepper sauce

2 sprigs thyme

2 stalks scallion/green onion (minced)

1 teaspoon allspice

½ teaspoon nutmeg

3 tablespoons soy sauce

¼ cup flour (for little dumplings)

2 quarts water (or enough to cover the cow's foot)

2 bay leaves

1 teaspoon curry powder

Place water, salt and cow's foot in a medium pressure cooker, cover and pressure for 10-15 minutes. Allow pressure cooker to cool down, check to see if meat is tender; then, add all the other ingredients, cover with foil paper or another cover, stir occasionally, season to taste. Simmer on low heat for about 25 minutes or until the gravy is thick and juicy. Serve with rice or any food of your choice.

Jerk Pork

Ingredients:

3 pounds pork leg cut in ½ inch pieces

½ cup soy sauce

2½ tablespoons Jerk seasoning

(use as desired)

½ teaspoon black pepper

¼ teaspoon thyme

2 tablespoons salt (or to taste)

½ teaspoon ground cloves

3 medium onions (diced)

8 cloves garlic (minced)

1 teaspoon cinnamon

1 teaspoon nutmeg

2 teaspoons grated ginger

1 teaspoon Scotch bonnet hot pepper sauce

2 tablespoons ground allspice

2 teaspoons sugar

3 bay leaves

In small bowl mix together all ingredients. Place pork pieces in a large bowl, then, add the seasoning. Next, use your fingers to rub the seasoning into pork.

Cover with plastic wrap and refrigerator for 12 to 24 hours. Preheat oven at 375° place all the meat along with seasoning in Pyrex baking dish, bake uncovered for 30 minutes then reduce heat to 350° cover with foil paper continue cooking for 20 minutes or until meat is tender and juicy. Gravy should be semi-thick, not watery. Remove from oven. Serve with white rice, rice and peas, festival, hard dough bread or hush puppies.

Oven Barbeque Ribs

Ingredients:

4 small slabs baby back ribs (pork)

1-8oz bottle barbeque sauce

1 teaspoon salt

½ teaspoon black pepper

Sprinkle ribs with salt and black pepper. Place ribs in a large plastic container and store in refrigerator for at least 4 hours. Remove from refrigerator and brush with barbeque sauce. Preheat oven to 325°. Wrap ribs tightly in foil paper and bake for about 2 hours or until tender. Remove from foil and add more barbeque sauce, if desired.

Roast Pork with Fresh Rosemary

Ingredients:

4-5 pounds pork leg

1 small onion (diced)

2 tablespoons scallion/green onion

(cut in small pieces)

1 teaspoon thyme

¼ cup teriyaki sauce

2 tablespoons Italian seasoning

1 teaspoon seasoning salt

1 teaspoon Scotch bonnet hot pepper sauce

½ teaspoon black pepper

6 cloves garlic (crushed)

3 sprigs rosemary

Place pork leg in large mixing bowl, in a small bowl combine all ingredients except rosemary, rub over meat using a sharp knife make small pockets in pork stuff seasoning in to pockets, cover bowl with foil paper place in refrigerator for at least 12 hours turning occasionally. Heat oven 375° place pork in Pyrex roasting dish, bake uncovered for about 40 minutes, reduce heat to 350° then add rosemary to dish cover with foil paper and bake for another 20-30 minutes or until pork is tender and juicy. Remove from oven slice and serve with white rice or rice and peas.

Bok Choy and Pork

Ingredients:

2 pounds pork leg (cut in cubes)

4 tablespoons soy sauce

½ teaspoon black pepper

¾ teaspoon seasoning salt

1 teaspoon Italian seasoning

½ teaspoon ground ginger

1 teaspoon thyme

1 small onion cut in chunks

1 teaspoon hot pepper sauce

2 tablespoons vegetable or coconut oil

1 medium bok choy vegetable

In large bowl combine pork and seasoning let sit for 1-2 hours or overnight. In large skillet heat oil and add pork without seasoning; stir. Cover and continue stirring periodically until pork is brown but not burnt; add a little water if needed and cook until tender. Next, add the seasoning and stir. Cut bok choy in 1 inch pieces and add to cooked pork then stir, cover and allow to simmer for 2-3 minutes. Serve hot with white rice.

Pork Chops with Beans

Ingredients:

4 boneless pork chops

2 tablespoons olive oil

½ cup chopped onion

½ cup celery

1 tin pork and beans

½ teaspoon black pepper

1 teaspoon seasoning salt

2 tablespoons brown sugar

Heat oil in medium skillet over medium to high heat and sprinkle pork chops with salt and pepper, then add to heated skillet cook for 15 minutes; turning from side to side until brown. Remove pork chops from skillet and set aside. Reduce heat to medium and add onion and celery. Cook until tender then stir in beans and brown sugar; bring to a boil. Return pork chops to skillet, cover and cook for 7 minutes.

Pig s Foot with Vegetables

Ingredients:

2 pounds Pig's feet

3 medium carrots (cut in 1 inch pieces)

1 medium onion (diced)

2 stalks scallion/green onion (minced)

½ teaspoon black pepper

1 teaspoon ground allspice

1 teaspoon salt (or to taste)

2 sprigs thyme

½ teaspoon Scotch bonnet hot pepper sauce

1 teaspoon curry powder

1 cho-cho (cut in small squares)

2 cloves garlic (minced)

3 tablespoons soy sauce

2 quarts water (or enough to cover the pig's foot)

Place water, salt and pig's foot in a medium size pressure cooker, and cook on high to medium heat for 15-20 minutes. Next, allow pressure cooker to cool, add chocho and other seasoning, cover with foil paper or any other cover (except the pressure cooker cover), cook on medium heat for at least 25 minutes, season to taste, stir occasionally or until the gravy is thick and juicy. Serve hot with white rice or food of choice.

Curry Goat

Ingredients:

3 pounds fresh goat meat

(cut in small pieces)

6 tablespoons curry powder or as needed

1 small onion (diced)

1 teaspoon thyme

6 cloves garlic (minced)

1 teaspoon seasoning salt

½ teaspoon black pepper

1 teaspoon Scotch bonnet hot pepper sauce

2 tablespoons soy sauce

2 tablespoons Italian seasoning

5 cups water or as needed

1 medium potato (cut in small squares)

In large mixing bowl season goat using your fingers to combine all ingredients except water rub together, let sit for at least 8 hour before cooking. In pressure cooker add water and seasoned goat cook for 10 minutes on medium heat, then remove from heat and cool, open pressure cooker and check if meat is tender, if not make sure enough water is in pressure cooker, continue cooking without cover until meat is tender. Add potatoes taste to make sure that it is seasoned to taste cover with foil paper or another cover and cook until gravy is thick and juicy. Serve with white rice, yellow or white yam, cooked green bananas, dasheen, breadfruit, cooked dumplings, or cooked cassava (yuka).

Chicken Stir Fry

Ingredients:

1 Large boneless/skinless chicken breast

(cut in small chunks)

2 pounds frozen stir fry mix

½ teaspoon chili powder

½ teaspoon black pepper

½ teaspoon Italian seasoning

½ medium onion cut in chunks

1 tablespoon soy sauce

2 tablespoons vegetable or coconut oil

Cut chicken breast in small chunks. In medium bowl combine chicken and all ingredients except oil and stir-fry set aside for about 20 minutes. Place skillet on medium heat, add vegetable oil and seasoned chicken; stir until chicken is cooked. Next, add the package of frozen stir-fry and sauce. Continue stirring until evenly coated. Cover and cook for 8 minutes on low heat. Serve with white rice.

Jerk Chicken

Ingredients:

3 pounds chicken (cut in small pieces)

2 tablespoons salt

½ teaspoon black pepper

2 tablespoon Jerk seasoning

(for extra or less use as desired)

½ cup soy sauce

3 medium onions (diced)

6 cloves garlic (minced)

2 teaspoon thyme

2 teaspoons ground allspice

2 teaspoons sugar

1 teaspoon cinnamon

1 teaspoon nutmeg

2 teaspoons grated ginger

1 teaspoon Scotch bonnet hot pepper sauce

¼ cup olive oil

Wash cut up chicken in water mixed with 2 tablespoons vinegar then, place in large mixing bowl combine all the ingredients using your fingers to rub together, cover and let it sit for at least 8 hours or overnight. In large Pyrex baking dish place the chicken with all the seasoning cover with foil paper. Preheat oven 350° place Pyrex in oven let cook for 25-30 minutes then remove foil paper taste to make sure seasoning is to taste, cook without foil for another 10 minutes stir together. You can also use stovetop for cooking. Gravy should be semi-thick not too watery. Serve with white rice, rice and peas, festival, or hard dough bread.

Fricassee Chicken

Ingredients:

1–3 pounds chicken (cut in small pieces)

4 tablespoons curry powder

1½ teaspoon seasoning salt

1 small onion (diced)

4 cloves garlic (minced)

3 sprigs thyme

2 bay leaves

1 teaspoon Italian seasoning

½ teaspoon black pepper

1 teaspoon Scotch bonnet hot pepper sauce

2 tablespoons soy sauce

1½cup water

2 tablespoons vegetables or coconut oil

1 medium potato cut in small squares

¼ teaspoon ground pimento

In large bowl combine chicken and all ingredients except water and vegetable oil. Rub together with fingers, let soak for at least 2 hours. Cook in large skillet or slow cooker over medium heat. Add oil when skillet is heated then add chicken and seasoning; stir, add water and cover, stirring occasionally. Steam for 20-30 minutes or until cooked; gravy should be thick. Taste to make sure there is enough seasoning. Serve with white rice.

Brown Stew Chicken

Ingredients:

2 pounds chicken breast boneless, skinless
(cut in chunks – small pieces)

½ cup onion (diced)

½ medium red bell pepper (cut in strips)

½ yellow bell pepper (cut in strips)

2 medium carrots (diced)

2 tablespoons vegetable or coconut oil

1 medium potato (diced)

½ teaspoon seasoning salt

½ teaspoon black pepper

2 celery stalks (diced)

2 tablespoons teriyaki sauce

1 teaspoon Italian seasoning

1 small tomato (diced)

2 tablespoons soy sauce

2½ cups water

¼ teaspoon allspice

In a large bowl wash chicken with lime juice, add all seasonings rub into chicken, set aside for about 50 minutes. Heat large skillet with oil remove the seasoning and vegetables from the chicken, place the chicken in hot oil cook until brown.

Then, add all the seasoning and vegetables to the skillet, stir together. Next, add water cover and steam, until completely cooked. Stirring occasionally until a thick and juicy gravy is achieved. Taste to make sure it is seasoned to taste. You may use slow cooker if desired. Serve with white rice or rice and peas.

Red Stripe Spicy Grilled Chicken

Ingredients:

2 pounds skinless, boneless chicken

½ cup Red Stripe Jamaican Lager beer

¾ cup soy sauce

½ cup vegetable oil

6 stalks scallion (minced)

1 Scotch bonnet pepper (seeded)

2 teaspoons fresh thyme leaves

¼ cup brown sugar

2 teaspoons nutmeg

2 teaspoons cinnamon

2 teaspoon ground clove

2 teaspoons allspice

Blend all ingredients in blender for about 10-15 seconds. Place chicken in a Zip lock bag and pour marinade in bag. Place bag in a shallow plate. Refrigerate 4-6 hours or overnight. Grill 4-5 minutes on each side, or until chicken cooked. Use a barbeque brush to quote chicken with the marinade.

Barbeque Chicken Jamaican Style

Ingredients:

3-4 pounds chicken cut in quarters

1 teaspoon seasoning salt

½ teaspoon black pepper

Dash of scotch bonnet hot pepper sauce. Rub seasoning on chicken 1 piece at a time, place in a bowl and let sit for about 1 hour before cooking. Cook chicken on a grill or in the oven at 350° or until fully cooked then use barbeque brush to coat chicken one piece at a time with barbeque sauce. Remove from grill or oven and apply sauce as needed.

Spicy Barbeque Sauce

Ingredients:

1 (8oz) bottle barbeque sauce

¼ cup ketchup

¼ cup soy sauce

¼ teaspoon black pepper

½ teaspoon Scotch bonnet hot pepper sauce

¼ teaspoon ground gloves

½ teaspoon ground ginger

¼ cup brown sugar

In medium mixing bowl combine all ingredients, use a barbeque brush, to quote chicken with sauce.

Creamy Baked Chicken

Ingredients:

3 medium size boneless chicken breasts

¼ cup grated sharp cheddar cheese

1-10oz can cream of chicken soup

¼ cup dry white wine

1 cup stove stop stuffing

¼ cup margarine (melted)

½ teaspoon salt

½ teaspoon black pepper

Sprinkle chicken breasts with salt and black pepper. Arrange chicken in baking dish and sprinkle with cheddar cheese. Mix soup with white wine and pour over chicken. Combine stuffing and melted margarine then sprinkle over chicken. Bake uncovered at 350° for 50 minutes or until cooked.

Stuffed Curry Chicken

Ingredients:

1 (4-5 pounds) chicken

½ cup chopped onion

½ cup chopped celery

¼ cup butter or margarine

1 teaspoon curry powder

½ teaspoon salt

½ teaspoon black pepper

5 cups dry bread cubes

1 cup chicken broth

Olive oil

Sprinkle the inside of the chicken with salt and black pepper, and place in a large bowl. Heat butter in a small saucepan then add chopped onions, celery, curry powder, dash of salt, and black pepper. Cook until tender then add bread cubes and enough chicken broth to moisten. Stuff chicken loosely with stuffing, tuck wings under, and tie legs together. Combine olive oil, dash of salt, curry, and pepper. Use a barbeque brush to brush the entire chicken. Place the chicken in roasting pan; heat oven to 375°. Roast uncovered for 2-2¼ hours or until cook.

Use drippings to base chicken occasionally until completely cooked.

Southern Fried Chicken

Ingredients:

1-4 pound chicken (cut in quarters)

1 teaspoon seasoning salt

1 teaspoon black pepper

3 eggs (beaten)

1 teaspoon Scotch bonnet hot pepper sauce

2 cups self-rising flour

1 tablespoon soy sauce

1 cup olive oil or coconut oil

In large mixing bowl season chicken with salt, black pepper, soy sauce, and hot pepper sauce; let sit for at least 2 hour. In another bowl combine flour, and a dash of black pepper. Heat deep fryer at 350° with coconut or olive oil. Whisk eggs with a dash of salt, hot pepper sauce and a little water. Dip each piece of seasoned chicken in egg mixture then coat with flour mixture and place in hot oil; fry until golden brown and fully cooked. Serve hot.

Herbal Roast Chicken

Ingredients:

1-4 pound roasting chicken

1 pack stove top stuffing

1 cup chicken broth

3 tablespoons butter

1 large onion (chopped)

¾ cup fresh chopped spinach

2 cloves garlic (minced)

2 teaspoons dried oregano

½ teaspoon dried rosemary

2 tablespoons half and half

2 tablespoons lemon juice

3 tablespoons olive oil

¼ teaspoon Italian seasoning

Preheat oven 350°. Wash chicken with lemon juice; pat dry with paper towels. In a large skillet, melt butter over medium heat, add onion, spinach, garlic, oregano, Italian seasoning and rosemary sauté for 5 minutes, then add chicken broth, and stove top stuffing to skillet; stir until well blended about 5 minutes. Next, add lemon juice and half and half to skillet and mix well. Place stuffing loosely in the cavity of the chicken. Tuck the wings under the chicken, place on roasting rack.

Roast chicken until the legs start to separate and chicken is golden brown.

Pineapple Chicken

Ingredients:

2 pounds chicken breast (cut in cubes)

1 teaspoon seasoning salt

2 tablespoons Kikkoman sauce

¼ cup La Choy sweet and sour sauce

1 cup frozen pineapple chunks

¼ cup ketchup

1 teaspoon thyme

1 teaspoon Italian seasoning

1 medium onion (cut in large cubes)

½ medium green bell pepper (cut in cubes)

½ medium yellow bell pepper (cut in cubes)

¼ medium red bell pepper (cut in cubes

½ teaspoon black pepper

2 tablespoons margarine

2 tablespoons olive oil

1 teaspoon grated or ground ginger

In large bowl combine chicken and all ingredients except: pineapple, sweet and sour sauce, and ketchup. In medium skillet on medium heat, add oil, when heated, add the seasoned chicken; stirring occasionally. Next, add ketchup and stir, then add frozen pineapple, and sweet and sour sauce, .mix well. Cover and cook for 10 minutes. Serve hot with rice.

Roast Chicken with Callaloo Stuffing

Ingredients:

1-4 pound chicken

1 teaspoon seasoning salt

½ teaspoon black pepper

3 tablespoon teriyaki sauce

½ teaspoon thyme

1 tablespoon margarine (melted)

½ teaspoon paprika

½ teaspoon Scotch bonnet hot pepper sauce

¼ teaspoon ground pimento

3 cloves garlic (crushed)

½ medium Onion (diced)

1 cup callaloo (drained)

Wash chicken with lime juice use a fork to clean the inside of the back. Mix salt, black pepper, teriyaki sauce, thyme, paprika, hot pepper sauce, and pimento. Rub seasoning on the inside and outside of chicken. Next, mix leftover seasoning with callaloo, onion and garlic, then, place the seasoned mixture in the cavity of the chicken, let sit for 2-3 hours or overnight. Preheat oven 350°. Place chicken in roasting pan, brush with melted margarine put in the oven and bake for 40 minutes, then, cover with foil paper and bake for another 15 minutes or until fully cooked and golden brown.

Apple-Glazed Chicken

Ingredients:

1-3 pound chicken (cut in quarters)

¼ cup apple sauce

1 tablespoon lemon juice

½ teaspoon ground allspice

1 small apple (cut in chunks)

½ teaspoon black pepper

1 teaspoon salt

2 tablespoon olive oil

2 tablespoons brown sugar

1 tablespoon margarine

Wash chicken and season with salt, and black pepper then brush with olive oil.

Preheat oven at 400°. Place chicken in baking pan and bake until golden brown and fully cooked. In a saucepan, over medium heat add margarine, applesauce; lemon juice, and allspice. Brush chicken with ½ the applesauce mixture. Reduce heat and continue cooking for an additional 10 minutes. Then, add apple chunks to the remaining applesauce mixture and cook for about 3 minutes. Place chicken on serving plate and pour apple mixture on top. Serve hot.

Apple Cinnamon Chicken

Ingredients:

2 large chicken breasts (cut in serving sizes)

2 tablespoons soy sauce

1 tablespoon teriyaki sauce

½ teaspoon black pepper

1 teaspoon dry parsley

1 tablespoon oregano

½ teaspoon salt

1 teaspoon cinnamon

1 tablespoon paprika

3 tablespoons La Choy orange ginger marinade

1 large apple (peeled and cut in chunks)

1 teaspoon brown sugar

½ medium green pepper (cut in chunks)

1 small onion (sliced)

1 tablespoon margarine

2 tablespoons olive oil

1 teaspoon lime juice

In a medium bowl, season chicken with soy sauce, teriyaki sauce, salt, and paprika. Cover and let sit for at least 30 minutes. Preheat oven 400°. Place chicken in a large Pyrex dish and cook for 35 minutes or until light brown. Next, in a medium skillet heat olive oil and margarine, add onion, green pepper, parsley, oregano and apple cook until tender. Then, add lime—juice, La Choy marinade, cinnamon and sugar, stir together. Cover and simmer for 2 minutes. Remove from heat pour over the chicken in Pyrex dish. Serve hot with rice.

Labor Day Chicken

Ingredient:

1-3 pound chicken (cut in small pieces)

1 teaspoon Italian seasoning

½ teaspoon black pepper

2 teaspoons curry powder

2 tablespoons soy sauce

1 tablespoon teriyaki sauce

½ teaspoon salt

½ teaspoon ground ginger

3 tablespoons ketchup

2 tablespoons fresh parsley (chopped)

2 teaspoons dry oregano

1 medium onion (cut in chunks)

½ medium green pepper (cut in chunks)

2 tablespoons margarine

¼ cup water

In a large mixing bowl combine chicken with Italian seasoning, black pepper, soy sauce, Curry powder, teriyaki sauce, ginger and salt, mix together well, set aside for at least 2 hours. Preheat oven at 350°. Place chicken in a Pyrex baking dish, let it cook uncovered for 60 minutes, turning the pieces. Next, add the onion, green pepper, parsley, oregano, ketchup, margarine and water, stir together. Then, cover with foil paper and steam for 15 minutes. Serve hot with rice or mashed potatoes.

Chicken with Broccoli

Ingredients:

1½ pound boneless chicken breast

(cut in cubes)

1 teaspoon olive oil

1-10oz can cream of chicken soup

½ cup evaporated milk

4 cups fresh broccoli florets

½ teaspoon seasoning salt

½ teaspoon black pepper

½ teaspoon Italian seasoning

2 tablespoon soy sauce

2 tablespoon olive oil

In mixing bowl season chicken with salt, black pepper, Italian seasoning, and soy sauce; heat oil in large skillet over medium-high heat. Next, add seasoned chicken and stir until cooked until slightly brown. Then, stir in cream of chicken soup, milk, and onion. Reduce heat, cover and cook for 5 minutes, next, add broccoli, cover and steam for 5 minutes. Serve hot with rice.

Honey Mustard Chicken Fingers

Ingredients: boneless, skinless, chicken breasts

(cut in ½ inch strips)

¾ cup all-purpose flour

½ teaspoon salt

½ teaspoon black pepper

¾ cup milk

1 cup olive oil for frying

Honey Mustard Sauce:

Ingredients:

½ cup honey ¼ cup mustard

Mix mustard and honey together and set aside. Combine flour, salt, and pepper in a plate, then, pour milk in a bowl. Dip chicken one piece at a time in milk roll in flour mixture coat well. Place chicken on parchment paper, preheat oil into large skillet over medium-high heat. Next place chicken in layers in hot oil. Fry, on each side for 2 minutes, or until golden brown and crisp. Drain on paper towel and serve with honey mustard sauce.

Roast Turkey

Ingredients:

1-10 or 12 pound turkey

2 ½ tablespoons kosher salt

2 teaspoons black pepper

2 teaspoons scotch bonnet hot pepper sauce

5 cloves garlic (crushed)

1 lemon cut in quarters

¼ cup soy sauce

2 tablespoons butter or margarine

2 cups celery diced

1 large onion cut in quarters

½ teaspoon ground cloves

1 teaspoon Italian seasoning

Wash turkey with vinegar put to soak overnight in water with 3 tablespoons salt. Next, mx all seasonings together, season inside and out of turkey. Then, mix together onion, celery, 2 cloves garlic place two pieces of lemon in the cavity of turkey. Place the crushed garlic and remaining lemon under the skin

Place turkey in roasting pan, brush with melted butter. Bake at 375° for 1 hour, basting occasionally with drippings from the turkey, when it is golden brown cover with foil paper, reduce heat to 350° and cook for another 50-55 minutes or until legs start to separate a little. Remove from oven and cool for 15 minutes before carving.

Gravy

Ingredients:

Drippings from the turkey and 2 tablespoons flour. Drain drippings into saucepan, mix flour in a little water and add to drippings stirring constantly for at least 2 minutes over medium heat.

Turkey Meat Balls

Ingredients:

1 pound ground turkey

1 teaspoon Italian seasoning

1 teaspoon seasoning salt

1 teaspoon black pepper

½ teaspoon dried parsley

3 tablespoons teriyaki sauce

1 teaspoon paprika

½ teaspoon onion powder

¾ teaspoon garlic powder

2 tablespoons olive oil

3 tablespoons seasoned bread crumbs

1 small onion (diced)

½ medium green pepper (diced)

¼ cup spaghetti sauce

2 tablespoons ketchup

½ teaspoon Italian seasoning

½ teaspoon oregano

1 small bay-leaf

½ teaspoon black pepper

½ cup water

In medium mixing bowl combine ground turkey, 1 teaspoon Italian seasoning, salt, 1 teaspoon black pepper, parsley, teriyaki sauce, paprika, onion powder, garlic powder, and bread crumbs mix together until fully combined then make small balls. Heat medium skillet with olive oil on medium heat, next add turkey balls about ½ inch apart. Cook until lightly brown, about 20 seconds on each side turning them regularly. When all the turkey balls are brown, next, add onions, bell pepper, spaghetti sauce, ketchup, black pepper, Italian seasoning, oregano, bay leaf and water. Stir together well, cover and cook on low heat until thick. Serve with freshly cooked spaghetti noodles.

Tasty Turkey Meat Loaf

Ingredients:

2 pounds ground turkey

1 small onion (diced)

3 cloves garlic (minced)

½ medium green pepper, (diced)

1 teaspoon ground cloves

½ teaspoon black pepper

½ teaspoon Scotch bonnet hot pepper sauce

3 tablespoons teriyaki sauce

2 tablespoon teriyaki sauce

½ teaspoon nutmeg

1 teaspoon seasoning salt

¼ cup ketchup

3 tablespoons

1 egg (beaten)

¼ cup breadcrumbs

1 teaspoon Italian seasoning

In large mixing bowl combine ground turkey, add all seasonings except 3 tablespoon ketchup mix with your fingers. In ungreased loaf tin place seasoned meat, flatten to form a loaf and even top. Bake for 30 minutes at 375°. Use pastry brush, to brush 3 tablespoons ketchup on top. Reduce heat to 350° bake for another 20 minutes. Slice and serve with mashed potatoes if desired.

Gravy

Ingredients:

1 tablespoon margarine

Dash of black pepper

Dash of salt

2 tablespoon ketchup

¼ teaspoon Italian seasoning

1 teaspoon paprika

In small saucepan heat margarine, add all ingredients and water stirring constantly for about 2 minutes.

Broiled Fish

Ingredients:

2 pounds fish of choice, (fillet or steak)

2 tablespoons butter or margarine (melted)

Salt and pepper as desired

Arrange fish in a single layer on a greased baking pan; melt butter or margarine brush ½ the melted butter over fish. Season fish to taste with salt and pepper, place baking pan with fish under broiler for 5 minutes; turn fish over and brush with remaining melted butter, broil for 5 minutes. Fish is done when flakey. Serve hot.

Sauteed Mackerel

Ingredients:

1 pack of salted mackerel (soaked, cooked and de-boned)

1 small onion, diced

½ teaspoon black pepper

2 tablespoons vinegar

¼ cup vegetable or coconut oil

1 small tomato diced

½ medium green pepper, (diced)

1 teaspoon hot pepper sauce

Boil mackerel in water, remove the bones (it should not be too salty) break in medium size pieces. Next heat skillet, then add vegetable or coconut oil, onion, tomato, and bell pepper. Allow it simmer for 1 minute then add mackerel, vinegar, black pepper, and hot pepper sauce; stir, cover for 1 more minute then remove from heat. Serve with cooked green bananas, yellow or white yam, dasheen, boiled plantains, cassava, dumplings, roasted breadfruit, or rice.

Mackerel Rundown

Ingredients:

1 pound mackerel (cooked, soaked and de-boned)

5 cups coconut milk (2 dried coconut created and juiced)

5 stalks scallions/green onions (cut in small pieces)

1 small onion (diced)

½ teaspoon curry powder

⅔ teaspoon black pepper

In large saucepan on medium heat, pour coconut milk and bring to a boil.

Reduce heat while skimming the cream and place into medium skillet. Only water should remain in the saucepan. Place skillet with coconut cream on medium heat and stir constantly; should now have custard and oil. Reduce heat, add curry powder, onion, scallion, mackerel, and black pepper; mix and remove from heat. Serve with rice, crackers, bread, boiled green bananas, fried dumplings or boiled dumplings.

Salt Fish with Butter Beans

Ingredients:

1 pack of salt fish (soaked, cooked and de-boned)

2—16 oz can butter beans (drained)

1 medium onion (diced)

1 medium green bell pepper (diced)

1 teaspoon black pepper

½ teaspoon hot pepper sauce

½ cup olive oil

Heat medium skillet over medium heat olive oil, onion, bell pepper, hot pepper sauce, and black pepper, stir together cook for 2 minutes, add salt fish stir, then add drained butter beans reduce heat to medium low, cover and steam for 5 minutes. Serve with rice or food of choice.

Ackee and Salt Fish

Ingredients:

1 pack salt fish (cooked and de-boned)

1-2 cans ackee (drained)

1 small onion (diced)

½ small green pepper, (diced)

½ teaspoon black pepper

1 small tomato (diced)

¼ teaspoon Scotch bonnet hot pepper sauce (optional)

¼ cup vegetable oil or coconut oil

Cook salt fish and soak in cold water to remove some of the salt (taste a piece to make sure it is not too salty). Break into small pieces. In medium saucepan heat oil then add ingredients; simmer for 2 minutes then add salt fish and stir. Next, add drained ackee, cover and simmer for 2 minutes. Remove from heat and serve hot with white rice, boiled dumplings, fried dumplings, bammy, Jamaican hard dough bread, boiled green bananas, boiled plantains, boiled cassava, yellow yam, dasheen or roasted breadfruit.

Jamaican Salt Fish Rundown

Ingredients:

1 pound salt fish (cooked, soaked and de-boned)

5 cups coconut milk (2 dried coconut created and juiced)

5 stalks scallions (diced)

1 small onion (diced)

½ teaspoon curry powder

⅔ teaspoon black pepper

In large saucepan on medium heat pour coconut milk and bring to a boil. Then lower heat while skimming the cream and place the cream into medium skillet. When skimming of the cream is finished and only water remains in the saucepan, put skillet with coconut cream on medium heat; stir constantly until you see custard and oil. Reduce heat and add curry powder, onion, scallion, salt-fish, and black pepper. Mix and remove from heat. Serve with rice, crackers, bread, boiled green bananas, fried dumplings or boiled dumplings.

Steamed Salted Fish

Ingredients:

1 pound pack salted cod fish (boiled, soak and deboned)

¼ cup olive oil

1 small onion (sliced)

1 small green bell pepper (cut in ½ inch chunks)

1 medium tomato (diced)

1 teaspoon black pepper

½ teaspoon Scotch bonnet hot pepper sauce (optional)

1 teaspoon Italian seasoning

½ teaspoon dried parsley

Boil salt fish, de-bone and soak in cold water (should not be overly salty).

Break the fish in small pieces and set aside. Taste a small piece to make sure it is not salty. Heat a medium size skillet over medium to high heat then add oil, onion, bell pepper, tomatoes, black pepper, Italian seasoning, parsley, and hot pepper sauce. Stir together, reduce heat, add salt fish, cover and simmer for about 5 minutes stirring a few times. Serve with boil bananas, fried dumplings, or rice.

Steamed Okra and Salt Fish

Ingredients:

1 pound salt fish (soaked, boiled and de-bone)

1 pound okra (trimmed and cut in medium size pieces)

1 medium onion (diced)

2 Roma tomatoes (diced)

1 tablespoon margarine

1 teaspoon black pepper

½ teaspoon Scotch bonnet hot pepper sauce

½ medium green bell pepper, (diced)

¼ cup olive oil

In a medium saucepan, boil okra until a little crunchy, boil salt fish, remove the bones and break into medium size pieces. Next, heat a medium skillet, and add oil, margarine, onion, bell pepper, tomatoes, black pepper and hot pepper sauce cook for about 3 minutes, or until tender. Then, add salt fish and okra, stir together, reduce heat, cover and simmer for about 10 minutes.

Spicy Salt Fish Fritters

Ingredients:

1 pound salt fish (cooked and de-boned)

2 cups flour

1 teaspoon baking powder

4-6 stalks scallion (green onion) cut in small pieces

1 small onion minced

3 cloves garlic mined

½ teaspoon black pepper

½ teaspoon curry powder

Dash of Scotch bonnet pepper or hot pepper sauce

Vegetable oil for frying

Water (use as needed)

Cook salt fish soak in cold water to remove most of the salt (if possible get boneless salt fish). After fish is cooked, break into small pieces. In large mixing bowl combine all ingredients, using a wooden spoon to mix all ingredients together. Add water to make a thick paste; it should be wet but not runny. Taste to make sure it is season to taste. In large skillet or deep fryer heat vegetable oil until very hot, add curry powder and stir. Then, use a spoon to drop batter in hot oil; reduce heat. Use a spatula to turn until both sides are golden brown. Serve warm or hot.

Steamed Red Snapper Fish

Ingredients:

2 pounds fresh red Snapper

(or fish of choice)

2 tablespoons butter or margarine

1 small onion cut in rings

2 sprigs thyme

2 tablespoons Kikkoman sauce

½ teaspoon black pepper

¼ teaspoon scotch bonnet hot pepper sauce

½ teaspoon seasoning salt

1 teaspoon Italian seasoning

3 tablespoons water

1 small tomato (diced)

In medium skillet place fish and all seasonings, water and butter or margarine.

Cover steam on medium heat for 10-15 minutes.

Escovitch Fish

Ingredients:

2 pounds small whole fresh fish or sliced fish (of choice)

½ cup vegetable or coconut oil

2 teaspoon salt

1½ teaspoon black pepper

1 Scotch bonnet pepper (remove most of the seeds cut in strips)

4 tablespoons vinegar

1 large onion (cut in rings)

Wash fish with lime or lemon juice, sprinkle with salt and black pepper on the inside and outside of each fish and place in a container; let it sit for at least 1 hour. Heat deep fryer or skillet with vegetable oil, place fish (one at a time) in hot oil, turn over to the other side until all fish is fried dry, remove and place on a platter. Cut onion in rings, cut pepper in small strips, then add onion and pepper in 4 tablespoons of the remaining oil in skillet or deep fryer, let it sauté for 1 minute then add vinegar stir together remove from heat and, pour over fish on the platter, make sure it is evenly distributed.

Brown Stew Fish

Ingredients:

2 pounds fresh snapper (or fish of choice)

1 teaspoon seasoning salt

1 teaspoon Italian seasoning

¾ teaspoon black pepper

1 medium onion (cut in chunks)

½ teaspoon Scotch bonnet hot pepper sauce

1 small tomato (cut in chunks)

½ medium green bell pepper (cut in chunks)

½ medium red bell pepper (cut in chunks)

2 cloves garlic (minced)

3 tablespoons vegetable or olive oil

2 tablespoons margarine or butter

3 tablespoons water

2 tablespoons soy sauce

Wash fish with lemon juice, sprinkle fish with salt and black pepper, heat medium skillet and add oil; cook until both sides of fish are light brown. Next, add seasoning, water, soy sauce, hot pepper sauce, and butter; cover and steam for 5-10 minutes. Remove from heat and serve hot.

Salmon Cooked in Red Wine

Ingredients:

1 pound skinless or skin on, boneless salmon

½ teaspoon black pepper

½ teaspoon seasoning salt or Mrs. Dash seasoning

½ teaspoon Italian seasoning

3 tablespoons red wine

Sprinkle salmon with salt, black pepper, or Mrs. Dash, and Italian seasoning. Heat oven at 350° then line cookie sheet with foil paper and place salmon on cookie sheet, bake for 6 minutes, 3 minutes on each side pour red wine over salmon and cover with foil paper. Cook for 1 additional minute. Remove from oven and serve. Salmon can be cooked in skillet on stovetop too.

Salmon with Caramelized Onions

Ingredients:

2—6oz salmon fillets

½ teaspoon black pepper

½ teaspoon paprika

1 tablespoon lemon juice

1 teaspoon garlic powder

1 teaspoon Mrs. Dash seasoning

¼ teaspoon salt

2 tablespoons olive oil

1 large onion (sliced in rings)

¼ teaspoon Scotch bonnet hot pepper sauce

2 teaspoon butter or margarine

1 teaspoon brown sugar

Combine black pepper, paprika, garlic powder, Scotch bonnet pepper sauce, Mrs. Dash, and salt in a small bowl; stir in 1 tablespoon of olive oil to make a paste. Sprinkle salmon with lemon juice, then, spread the paste over the salmon fillets and set aside to marinate for 10 minutes. Preheat oven on broil, place salmon on a cookie sheet lined with foil paper, next place cookie sheet directly under the broiler. Broil for about 6 minutes or until sizzling. Turn oven off, remove salmon to serving plate. Next, in a small skillet heat the remaining olive oil and margarine over medium heat, stir in the onion and sugar cook until tender and golden brown. Pour the caramelized onions over salmon fillets and serve.

Spicy Boiled Crawfish

Ingredients:

6 pounds live crawfish

1 gallon water

2 stalks celery (cut in quarters)

2 large onion (cut in quarters)

2 lemons (cut in quarters)

½ cup salt

10 whole pimentos

4 cloves garlic (minced)

3 bay leaves

1 tablespoon crushed red pepper

1 teaspoon Scotch bonnet hot pepper sauce

1 teaspoon dried thyme

½ teaspoon cayenne pepper

Melted butter or margarine, as desired

Wash crawfish in cold water. In large pot combine water, bay leaves, lemons, salt, celery, pimentos, garlic, red pepper, thyme, Scotch bonnet hot pepper sauce, and cayenne pepper. Bring to a boil, add crawfish, and cook for about 5 minutes or until crawfish turn deep red; cool and drain water from crawfish. Serve with melted butter. The broth is good to drink.

Spicy Jamaican Crab Cakes

Ingredients:

1 egg (beaten)

½ cup finely crushed saltine crackers

⅓ cup milk

½ teaspoon dry mustard

⅛ teaspoon white pepper

⅛ teaspoon cayenne pepper

7 ounces crab meat

1 tablespoon minced parsley

3 tablespoons unsalted butter

Lemon wedges for garnish

½ teaspoon dry jerk seasoning

¼ teaspoon Scotch Bonnet hot pepper sauce

In a bowl combine beaten egg, crackers, milk, mustard, white pepper, and cayenne pepper. Stir in crabmeat and add parsley. Shape into patties using ½ cup of mixture for each patty. Cover and chill for at least 30 minutes. Heat skillet with butter and add crab cake patties; cook over medium heat for 6-8 minutes on each side or until golden brown. Serve with lemon slices.

Mo-Bay Curry Shrimp

Ingredients:

2 pounds peeled shrimps

½ teaspoon black pepper

½ teaspoon seasoning salt

4 tablespoons curry powder

1 teaspoon Scotch bonnet hot pepper sauce

2 tablespoons vegetable oil

½ teaspoon Mrs. Dash

¼ cup water

1 teaspoon thyme

½ medium onion diced

1 tablespoon margarine

2 cloves garlic minced

In mixing bowl combine shrimp and all seasoning, let sit for 20 minutes. In large skillet over medium heat, heat oil then add seasoned shrimp; stir. Next, add water and margarine, cover and steam for 5-10 minutes; stirring occasionally. Serve hot with white rice.

Shrimp Fried Rice

Ingredients:

2 cups white rice (cooked and cool)

1 pound small cooked shrimps

1 small onion (diced)

4 tablespoons soy sauce

3 stalks scallions/green onion

(cut in small pieces)

¼ teaspoon black pepper

2 eggs (beaten)

2 tablespoons margarine

Dash of hot pepper

In large skillet on medium heat, heat margarine sauté onions and shrimps for 1 Minute add black pepper, hot pepper sauce and cooked rice, stir to coat rice. Next, add eggs and soy sauce stir until rice is completely coated and heated. Then add scallion and stir again. Remove from heat. Serve hot.

Curried Lobster

Ingredients:

2 pounds lobster tail

4 tablespoons curry powder

1 teaspoon seasoning salt

½ medium onion diced

1 teaspoon Mrs. Dash

½ teaspoon black pepper

½ teaspoon hot pepper sauce

1 tablespoon butter

½ teaspoon thyme

2 cloves garlic minced

¼ cup water

2 tablespoons vegetable oil

Cut lobster in small pieces, put in large bowl with all seasoning and mix together; let sit for 20 minutes before cooking. In large skillet heat oil and add seasoned lobster; stir, then, add water. Stir again and cover; steam for 10–15 minutes. Serve hot with white rice.

Barbeque Baked Beans

Ingredients:

1 (28oz) baked beans

¼ cup Hungry Jack pancake syrup

1 tablespoon brown sugar

½ teaspoon hot pepper sauce

Dash black pepper

½ cup barbeque sauce

In medium saucepan combine, all ingredients on medium heat bring to a boil.

Pour in Pyrex dish and bake for 15-20 minutes at 350°. Serve with Barbeque Chicken.

Bacon Green Beans

Ingredients:

6 slices bacon (crumbled)

3 tablespoons butter

½ cup red onion (chopped)

2 pounds fresh green beans (trimmed and cut in halves)

1 large clove garlic (minced)

¼ cup chicken broth

1½ teaspoon white balsamic vinegar

Salt and pepper to taste

Cook bacon over medium heat until crisp and drain on paper towel. Melt butter in skillet over medium heat, add onion, cover and simmer until tender.

In saucepan cook green beans with a dash of salt until tender. Drain green beans and add to onion, stir in bacon, garlic, and chicken broth. Bring to a boil.

Cover and simmer over low heat for 10 minutes. Sprinkle with salt, and pepper.

Serve hot.

Steamed Vegetables

Ingredients:

4 medium Carrots (sliced)

2 medium turnips (sliced)

1 pack frozen Green beans

12 medium Ecru (cut in two)

2 tablespoons butter or margarine

Dash of salt

½ teaspoon black pepper

2 tablespoons water

Slice carrots in oblong, inch pieces, cut turnips in chunks, thaw frozen green beans cut each ecru in two pieces. In medium skillet over medium heat place carrots, green beans, ecru, turnips, black pepper, dash of salt, margarine and water. Cover and steam for 3 minutes or until tender.

Bacon Eggplant

Ingredients:

5 slices bacon (pork or turkey)

1 medium onion chopped

1 medium eggplant (peeled and cut into ¼ inch strips)

1 8oz can tomatoes (undrained)

2 tablespoons parsley (chopped)

1 teaspoon sugar

¾ teaspoon dried basil

½ teaspoon salt

Dash of black pepper

In skillet cook bacon until crisp. Remove from skillet crumble and set aside. Reserve 2 tablespoons of bacon drippings; cook onion in drippings for 5 minutes or until tender. Stir in bacon, eggplant, undrained tomatoes, sugar, basil, salt, and black pepper. Cover and simmer for 10 minutes. Place eggplant mixture into serving dish and top with parsley. Serve hot.

Sweet and Sour Coleslaw

Ingredients:

5 cups shredded green cabbage

⅓ cup finely chopped onion

½ cup mayonnaise or salad dressing

2 tablespoons sweet pickled relish

1 tablespoon sugar

1 tablespoon vinegar

½ teaspoon salt

½ teaspoon celery seed

In a large bowl combine the cabbage and onion; set aside. Prepare the dressing by mixing mayonnaise or salad dressing, pickled relish, sugar, salt, vinegar and celery seed; stir until the sugar is completely dissolved.

Pour the dressing over the cabbage mixture, toss lightly to coat vegetables.

Chill and serve.

Cabbage Apple Slaw with Butter

Ingredients:

1 small granny apple (cut in cubes)

½ medium Cabbage (thinly sliced)

1½ teaspoons fresh lemon juice

1½ teaspoons unsalted butter

2½ teaspoons sugar

1½ tablespoons chopped fresh chives

Peel and cut apple into ½ inch cubes, sliced cabbage thinly about 3 cups. In a bowl toss the apple, cabbage, lemon juice, sugar and salt to taste., then, melt butter over medium heat in a skillet, add butter and chives to cabbage mixture and toss.

Roast Corn on the Grill
or In the Oven

Ingredients:

3 ears corn in the husk

Place corn on the grill or in the oven in the husk turn the corn constantly until corn is steamed. Using an oven glove pull back the husk, and return to oven or grill for another 4 minutes while turning so that heat is evenly distributed and a little blackened.

Creamy Potato Salad

Ingredients:

2 pounds new red potatoes (peeled and cut in ½ inch cubes)

¾ cup Caesar Dressing

½ cup grated Parmesan cheese

¼ cup freshly chopped parsley

¼ cup chopped red peppers

¼ cup chopped yellow peppers

Cook potatoes for 10-15 minutes or until tender. Place potatoes in a large bowl. Pour Caesar dressing over potatoes; add cheese, parsley, red and yellow peppers and toss lightly. Serve warm or chilled.

Baked Potatoes

Ingredients:

4 medium baking potatoes

½ cup sour cream

½ teaspoon salt

1 tablespoon sliced scallion

1 tablespoon butter (optional)

Scrub potatoes thoroughly with a vegetable brush. In medium saucepan, boil potatoes for 10 minutes. Then, wrap potatoes in foil paper and bake at 425° for 15-20 minutes or until crisp. Slice potatoes lengthwise on the top of each potato. Mix sour cream and salt then place in potatoes and top with sliced scallion. Serve With butter.

Garlic Cheese Mashed Potatoes

Ingredients:

1 pound Irish potatoes

¼ cup milk

¼ cup cheese

3 tablespoons butter or margarine

1 teaspoon garlic powder

In a medium saucepan with water and salt, peel and boil potatoes until tender.

Place potatoes into a bowl then add butter, cheese, garlic powder, and milk; use a potato masher to mash potatoes until smooth and creamy. Serve warm.

Garlic Red Potatoes with Parsley

Ingredients:

1. pounds small red potatoes, (scrubbed)

1 tablespoon olive oil

1 medium onion (chopped)

2 cloves garlic (crushed)

1 cup chicken broth

1 cup chopped fresh parsley

½ teaspoon black pepper

Wash potatoes and place in a bowl of cold water and set aside. Heat a large skillet over medium to high heat. Add olive oil, garlic, and onion sauté for 3 minutes or until tender. Next, add chicken broth and ½ cup parsley to skillet, stir and bring to a boil. Place potatoes in skillet. Reduce heat and continue cooking. Cover and simmer for 10 minutes or until potatoes are tender. Remove potatoes from skillet and place in a serving bowl, add black pepper to skillet, stir and pour over potatoes. Sprinkle the remaining ½ cup of parsley over the potatoes, and serve.

Oven Baked Potatoes with Herbs

Ingredients:

12 very small potatoes (washed)

4 teaspoons butter

¼ cup freshly chopped parsley

4 teaspoons fresh chives (minced)

¼ teaspoon black pepper

½ cup grated sharp cheddar cheese

Wash potatoes, place potatoes in water with a little salt in medium

Saucepan, make sure the water covers the potatoes. Boil over medium to high heat for 20 minutes or until potatoes when pierces with a fork is cook but firm. Remove potatoes to a baking dish. In a small saucepan melt butter, stir in chopped parsley, chives and black pepper. Pour over potatoes, sprinkle with cheese bake for 15 minutes or until cheese is melted. Serve hot.

Scalloped Sweet Potatoes

Ingredients:

3 large sweet potatoes (peeled and cut in round slices)

1½ cup heavy cream

1¼ cup shredded Swiss cheese (or cheese of choice)

½ teaspoon nutmeg

½ cup parmesan cheese,

Salt and pepper to taste

In a medium saucepan on medium heat, combine heavy cream 1 cup of shredded Swiss cheese, nutmeg, salt and pepper. Cook for about 5 minutes; stirring constantly. Preheat oven 400°. In a buttered casserole dish, add a layer of sliced sweet potatoes, then a layer of heavy cream mixture, repeat until the potatoes and mixture are finished. Sprinkle the remaining cheese. Place casserole on a cookie sheet and bake for 45 minutes or until potatoes are cooked and golden brown. Serve as a side dish.

Homemade Creamy Mashed Potatoes

Ingredients:

3 pounds potatoes (peeled and cut in two)

1½ cups half and half

4 cloves garlic (mashed)

1 cup sour cream

6 tablespoons butter (softened)

¼ cup scallions, thinly sliced

1 cup Italian bread crumbs

½ teaspoon black pepper

½ cup grated parmesan cheese

Salt to taste

In a large pot with cold salted water, add potatoes and bring to a boil, until cooked, mash potatoes with potato masher. In a small saucepan combine half and half and garlic over medium heat and bring to a boil. Then, remove from heat and take the garlic out. Next, add sour cream, black pepper, and scallion to mixture.

Next, add to mash potatoes and mix well until creamy. Pour potato mixture into a baking dish. In small bowl mix together breadcrumbs and parmesan cheese, spread over potato, dot with little pieces of butter and bake at 375° for 20 minutes or until golden brown.

Sweet Potato Cranberry Nut Dish

Ingredients:

2 pounds sweet potatoes (cut in cubes)

⅓ cup brown sugar

2 tins whole cranberry sauce

½ cup raisins

1 cup chopped almonds or walnuts

½ teaspoon salt

2 tablespoons margarine

¼ cup pineapple juice

2 teaspoons cinnamon

Preheat oven 350°. In large Pyrex dish arrange peeled cubed potatoes in layers; add a layer of cranberry sauce, sprinkle with sugar, cinnamon, raisins, nuts and salt, then repeat the process until it is all gone. Place small pieces of margarine all over the top; drizzle with pineapple juice. Bake uncovered for 45 minutes then cover and bake for another 15 minutes. Serve hot.

Sweet Potatoes with Coconut and Marshmallows

Ingredients:

40oz can sweet potatoes in syrup, drained (yams)

1 pack strawberry marshmallows

1 small pack shredded coconut

2 tablespoons margarine

2 tablespoons cinnamon

¼ cup brown sugar

¼ cup orange marmalade

¼ cup pineapple juice

Place the drained potatoes in Pyrex dish. Then, spread sugar and marmalade over potatoes Sprinkle cinnamon and coconut over the potatoes, next add small pieces of margarine, pineapple juice and carefully arrange marshmallows on top. Heat oven at 350° bake for 25-30 minutes or until heated and marshmallows are golden brown.

Fried Ripe Plantain

Ingredients:

1 Ripe Plantain 2 Tbs. olive oil

Use a knife to core the plantain straight down the side, then, remove the plantain and slice in round or oblong pieces. In a medium skillet heat 2 tablespoons oil, and place the plantains in the skillet about ⅛ inch apart, over medium heat, for about 30 seconds on each side or until they are golden brown, but not burnt. Remove from skillet and place on paper towel. Serve warm with meals.

Boil Green Bananas

Ingredients:

6 fingers green bananas

1 teaspoon salt

4 cups water

In medium saucepan place salt and bananas before doing so use a sharp knife to core both sides of bananas, boil for at least 10 minutes or until soft then remove skin with a fork; may be served with ackee and salt fish or sauteed mackerel.

Fried Breadfruit

Ingredients:

2 tablespoons olive oil

1 tablespoon margarine

6 thin slices of roasted breadfruit

In a medium skillet, over medium heat, heat oil and margarine, add the slices of breadfruit. Fry for about 30 seconds on each side or until golden brown. Remove from skillet and serve.

Roast Breadfruit

Breadfruits can be bought in Jamaican grocery stores or Asian food markets.

Make sure the breadfruit is fully developed and fit for roasting. Use a knife to take the stem out. Preheat oven to 400°. Place breadfruit on a piece of foil in the middle of the oven, bake until a knife is easily inserted in the breadfruit.

An exact time cannot be placed when it will be done, because it all depends on the size of the bread fruit. When breadfruit is baked allow to cool then use a sharp knife to peel it. Cut the breadfruit in quarters and remove the middle, slice into small slices and serve. or it can be fried and serve. Breadfruit can also be roasted on the grill.

Fried Bammy

Ingredients:

1 pack bammy (can be bought in Jamaican
Grocery stores)

¼ cup milk

2 tablespoons butter or margarine

1 tablespoon hot water

1 tablespoon olive oil

Cut each bammy in 4 pieces, place in a shallow dish and pour the milk over it. Let it soak in the milk for at least 5 minutes. Next, heat a large skillet with olive oil and 1 tablespoon butter, place bammy in the hot oil until both sides are brown, placing a little piece of butter when needed. When all the pieces are brown lower the heat, pour the water around the sides of the skillet, cover and steam for 1 minute. Remove from heat and serve hot.

Fried Dumplings (Johnny Cake)

Ingredients:

2 cups all-purpose flour

1½ teaspoon baking powder

Water as needed

¼ teaspoon salt

¼ cup vegetable oil

In medium mixing bowl combine flour, baking powder, and salt, add water and kneed with fingers adding a little water at a time. Kneed, until it all comes together and dough is slightly sticky. Roll dough into two pieces, then separate into small pieces and roll around in hand middle, then flatten with fingers. In medium skillet heat oil on low to medium heat then add dumplings after about 30 seconds keep turning them until completely fried, use a fork to test if ready, if fork pierce easily dumplings are ready.

Seasoned Turn Cornmeal

Ingredients:

2 cups yellow cornmeal

2 cups coconut milk

½ teaspoon black pepper

1¼ teaspoon seasoning salt

3 tablespoons margarine

1 teaspoon thyme

1 teaspoon Italian seasoning

1½ cup water

Dash of hot pepper sauce

1 small onion (diced)

4 stalks scallion (sliced in small pieces)

Combine water, coconut milk, salt, black pepper, onion, scallion, thyme and hot pepper sauce in medium saucepan bring to a boil on medium to low heat. Mix cornmeal with ½ cup water and pour into saucepan stirring constantly so that mixture will be smooth and moist. When cornmeal is smooth if needed add a little more water, cover stir occasionally. Reduce heat to low and steam for 10 minutes.

Serve hot.

Cinnamon French-Toast

Ingredients:

1 large egg

2 egg whites

¼ cup milk

¼ teaspoon vanilla extract

½ teaspoon cinnamon

½ teaspoon nutmeg

8 slices 1-inch thick bread (of your choice)

Cooking spray

In a shallow bowl, using a wire whisk or a fork beat the egg and egg whites until foamy. Add the milk, vanilla, cinnamon, and nutmeg. Wisk well and set aside.

Preheat oven to 200°F. Lightly spray a large non-stick skillet with olive oil cooking spray, heat over medium heat. Dip each slice of bread into the egg mixture, turning to coat and draining excess back into the dish and repeat the process until completed. Place bread slices in skillet cook until golden brown turning once, about 1-2 minutes. Transfer cooked slices to a serving plate; keep warm in the oven. Sprinkle lightly with cinnamon sugar and serve with syrup of choice.

Stovetop Stuffing Outside the Turkey

Ingredients:

2 packs Stovetop stuffing mix

2 cans Swanson chicken broth

1 cup celery (diced)

1 medium onion (diced)

¼ teaspoon black pepper

1 tablespoon margarine

¼ cup evaporated milk

¼ cup raisin

In medium skillet melt margarine add celery black pepper and onions, sauté for 2 minute, then, add chicken broth bring to a boil. Next, add stove top stuffing, raisins, and evaporated milk mix well. Place in baking dish and bake at 350° for 15-20 minutes.

Delicious Hush Puppies

Ingredients:

1 cup buttermilk

2 tablespoons water (if needed)

½ cup finely chopped onion

1¾ cup cornmeal

½ cup all-purpose flour

1 tablespoon sugar

2 teaspoons baking powder

1 teaspoon salt

½ teaspoon baking soda

Cooking oil for frying

Combine buttermilk, onion, and water; set aside. In large mixing bowl combine cornmeal, flour, sugar, baking powder, salt and baking soda. Add buttermilk mixture to cornmeal mixture, stir until moisten; Kneed slightly should be a little sticky, roll small pieces into balls, place in hot oil and deep fry for 2 minutes or until golden brown, turning once. Serve hot.

Grilled Cheese Sandwich with Onions

Ingredients:

6 slices whole wheat bread

2½ tablespoons butter or margarine (softened)

½ medium onion minced

3 slices cheese

3 tablespoons crated cheddar cheese

In small skillet with ½ tablespoon margarine sauté onion, butter the bread on both sides, heat medium skillet on medium heat, put bread in skillet for 5 seconds turn over for another 5 seconds repeat until all 6 slices are done. Place 1 slice of cheese on each slice of bread spread onion and grated cheese put the other slices of bread on top makes 3 sandwiches. Preheat griddle at 350°. Place sandwiches on griddle, heat for 5 minutes turning from side to side until completed. Serve hot.

Festivals

Ingredients:

1½ cups flour

3 tablespoons cornmeal

¾ cup water

½ teaspoon salt

3 tablespoons brown sugar

1 teaspoon baking powder

1 teaspoon vanilla

Vegetable or coconut oil for frying

In a large bowl sift flour and cornmeal together, stir in salt, sugar and baking powder. Then, add vanilla, and water as needed in small amounts, use your fingers to mix well, until dough is formed, it should be slightly sticky if the mixture gets too wet add a little more flour, until it is right. Cover the dough and let sit for 30 minutes. Divide the dough into 6 pieces; knead each piece, and roll into sausage like shape. Next, roll each piece into small balls and coat with flour, cornmeal and salt mixture. Pour oil into deep fryer, and fry until golden brown. Served with all Jamaican dishes.

Seasoned Macaroni and Cheese

Ingredients:

1-8oz pack elbow Macaroni

¼ cup water from macaroni

3¼ cup grated cheddar cheese

¼ cup cheddar cheese

2½cup evaporated milk

2 teaspoons margarine

1 medium onion (diced)

1 medium green bell pepper (diced)

1 medium red bell pepper (diced)

1 medium yellow bell pepper (diced)

½ teaspoon black pepper

½ teaspoon Italian seasoning

½ cup cottage cheese

½ teaspoon hot pepper (optional)

¼ teaspoon salt

Cook macaroni as directed put cooked macaroni in large bowl. In medium saucepan combine milk, cheddar cheese, cottage cheese, salt and black pepper. Bring to a boil, pour into bowl with macaroni, mix well. Then, add onions, bell pepper, hot pepper sauce, margarine, water and Italian seasoning mix well. Pour into Pyrex baking dish sprinkle with ¼ cup cheddar cheese and bake at 355° for 50-60 minutes.

Seasoned Rice

Ingredients:

2 cups white rice

1 small onion diced

2 stalks scallion/green onion (cut in small pieces)

¼ teaspoon black pepper

¾ teaspoon seasoning salt

3 tablespoons margarine

½ teaspoon Scotch bonnet hot pepper sauce

1 cup coconut milk

1½ cup water

½ teaspoon thyme

Wash rice about three times in cold water, combine all ingredients in medium saucepan on medium to low heat cover and steam until rice is cooked stirring occasionally. Rice should be fluffy. Serve hot. Rice cooker can be used.

Pumpkin Rice

Ingredients:

2 cups pumpkin diced

2 cups coconut milk

2 tablespoons margarine

2 cups rice

1 teaspoon thyme

½ teaspoon hot pepper sauce

1 teaspoon seasoning salt

½ teaspoon black pepper

1 cup water

In medium saucepan over medium heat, combine all ingredients except rice, bring to a boil cook for 10 minutes. Use a fork to crush pumpkin wash rice 3 times then add to saucepan, cover reduce heat to low and cook for 10 minutes or until rice is cook and shelly.

Seasoned Rice with Corn

Ingredients:

8oz pack frozen corn

2 cups coconut milk

2 cups rice

1 small onion minced

2 tablespoons margarine

1 teaspoon thyme

1 teaspoon seasoning salt

¼ teaspoon hot pepper sauce

1 small green bell pepper diced

2½ cups water

½ teaspoon black pepper

In medium saucepan over medium heat combine coconut milk, water, frozen corn, onion, thyme, bell pepper, hot pepper, margarine, salt, and black pepper, bring to a boil. Then, wash rice at least 3times add to saucepan cover and cook for 10 minutes, over low heat cook for 10 minutes or until rice is cooked and fluffy.

Rice and Peas

Ingredients:

2 cans red peas or pinto beans

1 cup coconut milk

3½ cups rice

¼ teaspoon black pepper

2 sprigs thyme

1¼ teaspoon salt

2 cups water

In large saucepan combine all ingredients on medium to low heat stir and cover to steam, taste to make sure seasoning is enough. Rice should be shelly NOT sticky. Rice cooker may be used also. When cook serve hot with meat of choice.

Rice with Green Peas

Ingredients:

1 (16 oz) can green peas (drained)

2 cups coconut milk

1 teaspoon seasoning salt

1 teaspoon thyme

I small onion diced

½ teaspoon black pepper

½ teaspoon hot pepper sauce

2 tablespoons margarine

1½ cups water

2 cups rice

In medium saucepan wash rice at least 3 times to get rid of some of the starch. Next, add drained green peas, coconut milk, water and all other seasonings. Cook over medium heat uncovered for 5 minutes, reduce heat to medium low, cover and cook for 10 minutes or until rice is cooked and fluffy.

Callaloo Rice

Ingredients:

¼ small onion diced

¼ small green pepper, (diced)

¼ teaspoon thyme

2 cups white rice

2 tablespoons margarine

2 cups coconut milk

1 cup callaloo drained (about ½ of a can)

½ teaspoon seasoning salt

½ teaspoon hot pepper sauce

½ teaspoon black pepper

1 cup water

In medium saucepan over medium to high heat; combine coconut milk, water, thyme, salt, onion, bell pepper, calalloo, black pepper, hot pepper sauce and margarine, bring to a boil on medium heat. Wash rice at least 3 times then pour into saucepan reduce heat, cover and steam for about 20 minutes or until rice is cooked and shelly.

Porridges

Banana Porridge

Ingredients:

2 fingers green bananas (grated)

3 tablespoons flour

¼ teaspoon salt

½ teaspoon cinnamon

¼ teaspoon nutmeg

½ teaspoon vanilla

¼ cup evaporated milk

½ cup condensed milk

4 cups water

Grate bananas mix with flour and a little water until smooth. In medium saucepan boil water salt vanilla, cinnamon, and nutmeg, then, add banana mixture, stirring constantly until smooth, add evaporated milk, (if too thick add a little more water or milk), cook for 8 minutes remove from heat and sweeten with condensed milk. Serve hot.

Cornmeal Porridge

Ingredients:

½ cup Quaker yellow cornmeal

¼ teaspoon salt

½ teaspoon vanilla extract

¼ teaspoon nutmeg

½ teaspoon cinnamon

¼ cup evaporated milk

½ cup condensed milk

5 cups water

In medium saucepan over medium heat boil water with salt, cinnamon, nutmeg, and vanilla, in small bowl mix cornmeal into a paste, pour into boiling water stirring constantly, so that it will not be lumpy, add evaporated milk and continue stirring, if it is thicker than you would like it add a little water or milk cook for about 3 minutes remove from heat and sweeten with condensed milk to taste. Serve hot.

Rice Porridge

Ingredients:

¼ cup white rice

2 tablespoons flour

¼ teaspoon salt

½ teaspoon cinnamon

¼ teaspoon nutmeg

½ teaspoon vanilla

¼ cup evaporated milk

½ cup condensed milk

3½ cups water

In medium saucepan cook rice in 3½ cups water. When rice is partially cooked mix flour in a paste add to rice stirring constantly so that porridge will not be lumpy, add evaporated milk, vanilla, nutmeg, and cinnamon (if it is too thick add water or milk) continue stirring, cook for 3 minutes sweeten to taste with condensed milk.

Plantain Porridge

Ingredients:

1 small green plantain (grated)

3 tablespoons flour

¼ cup evaporated milk

½ cup condensed milk

¼ teaspoon salt

½ teaspoon vanilla

¼ teaspoon nutmeg

½ teaspoon cinnamon

3-4 cups water

Grate plantain put in small bowl add flour and a little water to make a paste until smooth. In medium saucepan boil water, salt, cinnamon, vanilla, and nutmeg add plantain mixture stir until smooth, add evaporated milk cook for 8 minutes. (If porridge is too thick add water or milk). Remove from heat and sweeten with condensed milk to taste.

Oats Porridge

Ingredients:

½ cup Quaker oats

2½ cups water

¼ teaspoon salt

¼ teaspoon nutmeg

½ teaspoon vanilla

¼ teaspoon cinnamon

¼ cup evaporated milk

¼ cup condensed milk

In medium saucepan bring water with salt, cinnamon, nutmeg, and vanilla to a boil, pour in oats while stirring so that it won't be lumpy stir for 2 minutes. Then, add evaporated milk, remove from heat and sweeten with condensed milk to taste.

Cream of Wheat

Ingredients:

¼ cup cream of wheat

¼ cup evaporated milk

¼ cup condensed milk

¼ teaspoon salt

¼ teaspoon nutmeg

½ teaspoon vanilla

½ teaspoon cinnamon

3 cups water

In medium saucepan bring water to a boil add salt, cinnamon, nutmeg and vanilla add cream of wheat stirring constantly so that it won't be lumpy. Next, add evaporated milk cook for 2 minutes, sweeten with condensed milk to taste.

Sauces & Seasonings Plus . . .

Jerk Seasoning

Ingredients:

½ teaspoon nutmeg

½ teaspoon allspice

½ teaspoon salt

½ teaspoon black pepper

2 tablespoons ground pimento

2 cups scallion/green onions (chopped)

2 medium onions (chopped)

2 Scotch Bonnet peppers (minced)

2 tablespoons vegetable or coconut oil

Puree all ingredients in blender for 40 seconds, pour into a jar and refrigerate.

This seasoning can be used on chicken, pork, fish and beef.

Scotch Bonnet Hot Pepper Sauce

Ingredients:

12 Scotch Bonnet Peppers (cut in quarters)

5 medium carrots (diced)

2 cho-cho (Peeled and diced)

3 cloves of garlic (minced)

2 teaspoons ground ginger

2 medium onions (diced)

10 whole pimentos (crushed)

½ cup vegetable oil

½ cup white vinegar

In medium skillet over medium heat, heat oil, add onions and stir for 2 minutes.

Then, add cho-cho, carrots, pimento, garlic, and ginger continue cooking for

5 minutes, next add vinegar and pepper cook for 10 more minutes. Remove from heat and cool for 10 minutes. Place onion mixture in blender and blend for 2 minutes or until smooth, pour into a jar and store in refrigerator.

Spicy Barbeque Sauce

Ingredients:

1 (8oz) bottle barbeque sauce

¼ cup ketchup

¼ cup soy sauce

¼ teaspoon black pepper

½ teaspoon Scotch bonnet hot pepper sauce

¼ teaspoon ground gloves

½ teaspoon ground ginger

¼ cup brown sugar

In medium mixing bowl combine all ingredients, use a barbeque brush, to brush barbeque sauce onto chicken.

Honey Mustard Sauce

Ingredients:

½ cup honey

¼ cup mustard

Mix mustard and honey together and set aside.

Egg Wash

Ingredients:

1 large egg

2 tablespoons water

Beat the egg and water together, if more is needed repeat the process.

Soups

Chicken Vegetable Soup

Ingredients:

2 pounds chicken leg quarters

(cut in small pieces)

4 medium carrots diced

3 stalks celery diced

¼ cup frozen corn

2 medium Irish potatoes cut in quarters

½ cup frozen green peas

3 stalks scallion cut in small pieces

2 sprigs thyme

½ teaspoon salt

¼ teaspoon black pepper

Dash of hot pepper sauce (optional)

1 pack grace chicken noodle soup mix

1 pound yellow yam (peeled and cut in small pieces)

Place chicken and all vegetables in large pot ⅔ full of water on medium to high heat. When chicken, vegetables, and yam are cooked, add chicken noodle soup mix and all the other seasonings; stir, taste to make sure it is season to taste. Serve hot.

Split Peas Vegetable Soup

Ingredients:

1 pack dry split peas

10 cups water

Ham bone or 2 ham hocks

1 large onion (chopped)

1 cube chicken bouillon

½ teaspoon salt or to taste

¼ teaspoon black pepper

1 cup sliced carrots

1 cup celery (chopped)

½ cup light cream

1 tablespoon butter or margarine

1 cho-cho (sliced in cubes)

Place split peas, water, ham bone or ham hocks, in medium pot; cook for 35 minutes on medium to high heat. Then, add onion, cho-cho, chicken bouillon, salt, and black pepper. Cook until meat and vegetables are tender stirring constantly. Remove ham bones and chop meat into small pieces.

Return meat to soup, add carrots, and celery; season to taste, cover and simmer for 20 minutes. Next, add light cream and butter, reduce heat, to low, cover and cook for 10 more minutes. Serve hot.

Split Peas Soup

Ingredients:

1 small pack split peas

½ cup coconut milk

½ teaspoon thyme

½ teaspoon black pepper

1 teaspoon salt (or to taste)

1 pound yellow yam (peeled and cut in small pieces)

1 cup all-purpose flour (use to make small dumplings)

2 stalks scallion (green onions)

½ teaspoon Italian seasoning

1 pound beef soup meat

2 medium carrots (sliced)

¼ cup celery

1 teaspoon garlic powder

¼ teaspoon Scotch bonnet hot pepper sauce

Wash peas and soup meat and place in a large pot ¾ full of water on medium to high heat. Cook peas and meat until tender, then, add yam, carrots, dumplings, celery, scallion, thyme, Italian seasoning, black pepper, garlic powder, hot pepper sauce and salt. Continue to cook until the yams and dumplings are fully cooked.

Then, add coconut milk and season to taste, soup should be semi thick. Reduce heat cover and simmer for 10 minutes. Serve hot.

Dumplings

Ingredients:

5 tablespoons of flour

Pinch of salt

Water

Put flour and salt in a small bowl, add water and knead it into dough, break into small pieces and roll between the palm of your hands and place in the pot.

Pumpkin Vegetable Beef Soup

Ingredients:

1 pound beef soup meat

1 pound pumpkin cut in cubes

(about 2 cups)

1 pack Grace chicken noodle soup mix

½ teaspoon salt or to taste

¼ teaspoon black pepper

2 stalks scallion

1 pound yellow yam (peeled and cut in small pieces)

1 cup all-purpose flour (for dumplings)

½ cup diced carrot

1 small turnip (diced)

½ cup celery

1 teaspoon Italian seasoning

1 cho-cho (chayote, peeled and sliced)

2 sprigs fresh thyme

1 teaspoon Scotch Bonnet hot pepper sauce

Place meat and pumpkin in a medium size pot ⅔ full of water boil for about 30 minutes over medium to high heat until meat is tender. Remove as much of the pumpkin as possible and use a fork or potato masher to mash it. Then, return it to pot. Next, add yellow yam, dumplings, cho-cho, carrots, turnip, scallion, celery, thyme, Italian seasoning and black pepper, continue cooking. Next, add Grace chicken noodle soup mix. Stir, reduce heat, cover and simmer for 20 minutes or until everything is cooked; season to taste. Serve hot.

Cream of Callaloo Soup

Ingredients:

2 cups coconut milk

1 cup evaporated milk

1 can calalloo (drained and puree in blender)

1 small onion (diced)

1 teaspoon thyme

1½ teaspoon seasoning salt

4 cups water

3 stalks scallion/green onion (minced)

½ cup Parmesan cheese (grated)

2 medium potatoes (peeled and cut in small squares)

½ teaspoon black pepper

2 bay leaves

Place callaloo and 1cup of water in blender, pulse for 20 seconds. In medium pot combine water, potatoes, onion, coconut milk, scallion, thyme, black pepper, bay leaves, and salt. Cook on medium to high heat, then, add callaloo, and cook until the potatoes are tender. Next, add evaporated milk, and cheese; stirring constantly season to taste. Remove from heat and serve hot.

Manish Water

Ingredients:

1 goat head (chopped in small pieces)

3 cho-chos (peeled and diced)

6 fingers green bananas (peel 5 bananas/cut 1 in small pieces with the skin)

1 green Scotch bonnet pepper

2 sprigs fresh thyme

3 stalks scallions/green onion (crushed)

1 pound yellow yam (peeled and cut in small pieces)

½ teaspoon black pepper

1 small onion (diced)

1 tin coconut milk

3 medium carrots (diced)

1 cup celery (diced)

Salt to taste

In a large pot ¾ full of water, place goat head, let it cook on medium-high heat for about 2 hours or until cooked and tender. Next, add all the ingredients, and season to taste; cover and cook on low heat for 50 minutes or until completely cooked. Stir the soup a few times, each time you stir remove the Scotch bonnet pepper, and then, return it to the pot. Serve hot.

Vegetable-Beef Soup

Ingredients:

2 pounds beef shank or soup meat

10 cups water

2 teaspoons salt

½ teaspoon dried oregano

¼ teaspoon black pepper

2 bay leaves

1 pound yellow yam (peeled and cut in small pieces)

3 tomatoes (peeled and diced)

2 medium potatoes (peeled and cubed)

1 cup frozen lima beans

1 cup carrots (sliced)

1 cup celery (diced)

1 medium onion (chopped)

½ teaspoon fresh thyme

In medium pot combine water, beef shank, salt, and oregano. Cook on medium heat for 90 minutes, then, reduce heat and skim excess fat; add carrots, celery, tomatoes, onion, thyme, bay leaves, potatoes, yellow yam, black pepper, and lima beans. Cover and simmer for 40 minutes on low heat; season to taste. Serve hot.

Fish Tea

Ingredients:

2 pounds small whole fish (of choice)

2 quarts water

4 green bananas (in the skin)

1 small cho-cho (cut in chunks)

1 green Scotch bonnet pepper

4 Sprigs thyme

2 cloves of garlic (crushed)

2 potatoes (peel, cut in quarters)

1 teaspoon salt (or to taste)

1 teaspoon black pepper

2 stalks scallion/green onion (crushed)

Wash fish with lime juice, and clean it to remove all the scales. In a medium pot, place water, fish, and salt cook for about 15 minutes, then, cut each banana in two and add to the pot; next add potatoes, scallion, thyme, garlic, cho-cho, scotch bonnet pepper, thyme and black pepper, season to taste. Cover and cook for 15-20 minutes. Stir, occasionally, remove the scotch bonnet pepper before stirring each time. Serve hot.

Red Peas Soup

Ingredients:

1 pack soup bones (beef)

1 small pack cube steak

1 (8oz) pack dried red peas

3 medium carrots cut in ½ inch pieces

1 tin coconut milk

2 teaspoon seasoning salt

2 sprigs thyme

2 stark scallion/green onions

(cut in small pieces)

¼ teaspoon black pepper

2 bay leaves

¼ teaspoon rosemary

2 medium potatoes (cut in quarters)

½ cup all-purpose flour (for dumplings)

1 medium sweet potato (cut in quarters)

1 pound yellow yam (peeled and cut in small pieces)

Water as needed

In large pot wash red peas pour water to ⅔ full let it soak for about 4 hours or more, wash soup bones, and cube steak, place with peas and cook on medium high or slow cooker until peas and meat are tender, then add carrots, yellow yam, potatoes, and dumplings. Next add scallion, thyme, bay leaves, rosemary, and black pepper. Cover and cook for 5 minutes then add coconut milk taste to make sure it has enough seasoning. Cover and simmer on low heat. Serve hot.

Dumplings

Ingredients

½ Cup all-purpose flour

Pinch of salt

Enough water to make dough

Place flour in small bowl with a dash of salt and a little water mix together until a little sticky and is able to roll in hand middle. Roll in small balls then press in the middle or roll in hand (Twizzlers).

Pepper Pot Soup

Ingredients:

1 tin coconut milk

1 pound yellow yam (peeled and cut in small pieces)

2 sprigs fresh thyme

6 dasheen heart leaves (cooked and crushed

1 cho-chos (peeled and sliced in strips)

1 large sweet potato (peeled and cut in medium size pieces)

1 green Scotch bonnet pepper

½ cup all-purpose flour (for dumplings)

½ pound salt beef (soaked to remove most of the salt)

½ pound salted pig's tail (soaked to remove most of the salt)

Salt to taste

½ teaspoon black pepper

2 stalks scallion/green onion

(crushed and chopped)

Water

In a medium pot ¾ full of water on high-medium heat. Combine salt beef, pig's tail and dasheen heart, after about 15 minutes, remove the dasheen heart, place in a bowl and crush it with potato masher, then, return it to the pot. Continue cooking for about 40 minutes or until the meat is tender. Next, add the sweet potato, dumplings, chocho and all other ingredients. Season to taste, stirring occasionally, for 30 minutes or until the soup thickens slightly. Remove for heat and serve hot.

Breads

Banana Pineapple Bread

Ingredients:

3 cups all –purpose flour

1 teaspoon baking soda

1 teaspoon salt

1 teaspoon cinnamon

1½ cup light brown sugar

1 cup olive oil

1 (8oz) can crushed pineapple

2 cups mashed bananas (very ripe)

¼ cup sour cream

3 eggs (beaten)

1 teaspoon vanilla extract

½ teaspoon nutmeg

Combine flour, baking soda, salt, cinnamon, and nutmeg in a large mixing bowl.

Add sugar, olive oil, crushed pineapple, bananas, sour cream, eggs, and vanilla. Mix all ingredients together with a wooden spoon. Preheat oven at 350°. Pour batter into greased loaf tin and bake for about 45 minutes or until tooth pick inserted comes out clean.

Banana Bread

Ingredients:

1 stick butter

1¾ cup all-purpose flour

1 cup brown sugar

2 eggs

1 teaspoon vanilla

1 teaspoon baking soda

½ teaspoon salt

2½ cups mashed bananas (very ripe)

½ cup sour cream

¼ teaspoon nutmeg

Preheat oven 350°. In a large mixing bowl mix butter, sugar, eggs, vanilla, and nutmeg until fluffy. Sift together flour, baking soda, and salt then add to butter mixture. Mix for about 30 seconds then add bananas and sour cream, mix well. Pour into greased loaf tin and bake for 40 minutes or until tooth pick inserted comes out clean.

Hard Dough Bread

Ingredients:

4 cups all-purpose flour

4 tablespoons margarine

1 tablespoon dry yeast

2 tablespoons granulated sugar

1 cup water

1½ teaspoon salt

In large mixing bowl, combine all the dry ingredients. Next, use your fingers to mix butter in the dry ingredients, then, add the water and mix well. Place dough on a floured surface, knead with the palm of your hand for about 10-15 minutes, then grease a large bowl and place the dough in it. Rotate the dough to make sure it is greased. Cover with a clean towel or paper towel, then, place the bowl in a warm area in the kitchen for at least 45 minutes. Punch the dough several times to get rid of excess gas. Roll the dough into a rectangular shape with a rolling pin. Next, roll the dough as tight as possible, folding all the corners; it should be in the shape of a log. Place the finished product on a cookie sheet, and allow it to rise for 35 minutes. Preheat oven at 375°, bake until bread is slightly brown.

Desserts

Spicy Jamaican Bun

Ingredients:

1 cup mixed fruits

1 cup raisins

½ cup cherries (cut in quarters

1½ cups brown sugar

4 cups flour

½ cup browning or burnt sugar

1 can evaporated milk

½ bottle Guinness stout

1 cup red wine

2 tablespoons red wine

½ teaspoon nutmeg

1 teaspoon vanilla

2 teaspoons cinnamon

4 teaspoons baking powder

½ stick butter or margarine (melted)

2 large eggs beaten

½ teaspoon salt

1 teaspoon lime juice

2 tablespoons Jamaican white rum

(100% proof)

In large mixing bowl add evaporated milk, sugar Guinness stout, nutmeg, salt, cinnamon, mixed fruits, raisins, and cherries. Then add flour and baking powder; mix together well then add beaten eggs, browning, 2 tablespoons red wine, rum and melted butter or margarine, mix until evenly distributed.

Prepare baking loaf tin by spraying with Pam or coating with butter, dust with flour. Pour batter into pans ⅔ full place 3 cherries on top of batter. Heat oven 350° and bake for 35-40 minutes or until tooth pick inserted comes out clean. Cool then pour red wine over buns. In small sauce pan bring to a boil ¼ cup sugar and ¼ cup water and use pastry brush to glaze buns, serve with cheese if desired.

Sweet Potato Pudding

Ingredients:

2 pounds sweet potatoes (grated)

1½ cups brown sugar

1 cup raisins

2 tablespoons butter or margarine

½ cup evaporated milk

1 can coconut milk

½ cup shredded coconut

2-3 cups flour

½ teaspoon salt

1 tablespoon vanilla

½ teaspoon nutmeg

2 teaspoons cinnamon

1 tablespoon Jamaican white rum

(100% proof)

1 cup water

Peal and grate potatoes. In a large mixing bowl combine coconut milk, evaporated milk, sugar, water, vanilla, rum, salt, nutmeg, and cinnamon; mix until sugar is dissolved, then add grated potato, shredded coconut and flour (one cup at a time); mix together until a thick consistency is achieved, when a wooden spoon stands up straight in the mixture, it is ready. Prepare baking Pyrex dish by coating with margarine or butter pour mixture into dish ¾ full.

Cover with file paper or Pyrex cover. Heat oven 375° bake for 30 minutes then reduce heat to 350° bake until a pointed knife inserted comes out clean.

Let cool and serve.

Grater Cake Supreme

Ingredients:

3 packs grated coconut

2-3 cups granulated sugar

1 teaspoon grated ginger

½ teaspoon nutmeg

Cherries for garnish

3 cups water

In medium saucepan combine water, ginger, nutmeg and sugar, stirring constantly on medium to low heat boil for about 10 minutes. Drop spoon full on cookie sheet or parchment paper, while stirring on low heat and adding a little water to keep it moist. Place a cherry in the middle.

Ducunoo (Blue Draaws)

Ingredients:

4 large green bananas grated

1½ cups dark brown sugar

2 cups low fat milk

1 cup grated coconut

1 teaspoon salt (or to taste)

2 teaspoons ground cinnamon

1 cup coconut milk

2 cups flour (or as needed)

1 teaspoon vanilla

Banana leaves (can be found in Asian grocery stores)

Combine all ingredients except flour in large mixing bowl, then, add flour (1 cup at a time). When mixed it should be like dough, you may add milk or flour to get it to the right consistency. Place banana leaves in microwave for 10 seconds or until wilted, cut in 4 inches squares, place ducunoo mixture in the middle then roll and tie with cord so that it stays together during boiling. In large saucepan bring water to a boil then place the completed product in hot boiling water; boil uncovered for about 30 minutes. Remove from heat and cool. Refrigerate until ready to serve.

Rice Pudding

Ingredients:

½ cup white rice

2 tablespoons granulated sugar

1 tin condensed milk

2 tablespoons flour (or enough to make it thick)

¼ teaspoon cinnamon

¼ teaspoon vanilla

Dash of salt

Dash of nutmeg

¼ cup evaporated milk

Cherries for garnish

Water as needed

Cook rice in water add salt, vanilla, nutmeg, and cinnamon mix flour to a paste.

Then add, to rice stirring constantly for about two minutes. Next, add evaporated milk, sugar and condensed milk, sweeten to taste, should be thick and creamy.

Pour into small Pyrex dishes and refrigerate, serve cold.

Coconut Rum Cake

Ingredients:

⅓ cup butter or margarine

⅓ cup shortening

1½ cup granulated sugar

3 cups all-purpose flour

1¼ tablespoon baking powder

¾ teaspoon salt

1⅓ cup milk

2 teaspoons vanilla extract

1 cup shredded unsweetened coconut flakes

4 large egg whites

2 tablespoons Jamaican white rum

(100% proof)

2 cups shredded sweetened coconut

In large mixing bowl, mix shortening and butter on medium speed. Gradually add sugar until smooth. Next, add flour, baking powder, and salt, then, add milk to mixture; mix well. Stir in vanilla, rum, and beaten egg whites and 1 cup coconut flakes, mix well. Pour batter into prepared baking pan. Bake at 350° for 25 minutes or until toothpick inserted comes out clean. Cool for 15 minutes remove from pan and cool on wire rack. Arrange cake on cake plate. Spread cream cheese frosting over cake and sprinkle with 2 cups shredded sweetened coconut.

Coconut Drops

Ingredients:

1 large coconut cut in small squares

1 pound brown sugar

1 ½ tablespoon grated ginger

2 teaspoons cinnamon

½ teaspoon nutmeg

¼ teaspoon salt

8 cups water

Cut coconut into small squares. Boil coconut, ginger, nutmeg, cinnamon, and salt into 8 cups of water for about 50 minutes, add sugar stirring constantly on low to medium heat until thick and moist. Use a spoon to drop mixture on wax paper or parchment paper, add a little water if needed to keep consistency moist.

Yummy Cassava Pudding

Ingredients:

2-3 Packs grated cassava (yuka)

1½ cups brown sugar

1 cup raisins

½ cup evaporated milk

1 can coconut milk

½ cup shredded coconut

2-3 cups all-purpose flour

½ teaspoon salt

1 teaspoon vanilla

½ teaspoon nutmeg

2 teaspoons cinnamon

1 tablespoon Jamaican white rum
(100% proof)

2 tablespoons butter or margarine

1 cup water

Place grated cassava in large mixing bowl add sugar, coconut milk, evaporated milk, water, vanilla, rum, cinnamon, and nutmeg. Next, add flour (one cup at a time) to make a thick consistency. This can be achieved by placing a wooden spoon in the middle of mixture if it stand firm consistency is ready. Prepare baking pan or Pyrex dish by coating with Pam or margarine. Then pour batter in greased pan and bake at 375° for 30 minutes, reduce heat to 350° and bake for another 20 minutes or until completely baked. Remove from oven and cool. Slice and serve.

Cornmeal Pudding

Ingredients:

3 cups cornmeal

1 ½ cups brown sugar

1 cup raisins

½ cup evaporated milk

1 can coconut milk

½ cup shredded coconut

¼ cup flour

½ teaspoon salt

1 teaspoon vanilla

½ teaspoon nutmeg

2 teaspoons cinnamon

2 tablespoons butter or margarine

1 tablespoon Jamaican white rum

(100% proof optional)

2 cups water (add more if needed)

In large mixing bowl combine all liquids and sugar, stir until sugar is dissolved.

Then add cinnamon, vanilla, salt, and nutmeg mix together add shredded coconut, and raisins, stir in cornmeal and flour; should be very liquid, since cornmeal will swell. Prepare baking pan or Pyrex dish with Pam or margarine pour mixture into greased pan or Pyrex. Bake at 375° for 15 minutes then cover, reduce heat to 350° and bake for another 40 minutes or until bake.

Ginger Bun

Ingredients:

2 cups all-purpose flour

2 teaspoons baking powder

½ teaspoon baking soda

1 teaspoon ground allspice

½ teaspoon nutmeg

2 tablespoons grated ginger root

2 teaspoons ground ginger

¼ cup butter, melted

1 cup light brown sugar

¼ cup evaporated milk

¼ cup dark molasses

2 large eggs, beaten

In a large mixing bowl combine flour, baking powder, baking soda, allspice, nutmeg, and ground ginger. Next, add melted butter, sugar, and grated ginger and set aside. In a small saucepan heat evaporated milk and molasses until combined stirring constantly it should not come to a boil. Remove from heat and pour into flour mixture, stir together until well blended, add beaten eggs and mix well. Preheat oven at 350°. Pour batter into baking pan and bake for 45 to 50 minutes or until toothpick inserted comes out clean. Remove from oven and cool on wire rack. Serve with white icing glaze if desired.

Icing Glaze

¼ cup powdered sugar

1 teaspoon lime juice

2 tablespoons water (water may be added if needed)

Mix water, lime juice and powdered sugar together over low heat, then, spoon over bun.

Toto

Ingredients:

1 coconut grated or I pack grated coconut

1½ cup brown sugar

3 cups all-purpose flour

1large egg beaten

1 teaspoon baking soda

1 teaspoon baking powder

1 teaspoon cinnamon

½ teaspoon nutmeg

1 teaspoon vanilla

½ teaspoon salt (or to taste)

2 tablespoons butter or margarine (melted)

2-2 ½ cups water or as needed

½ cup evaporated milk

1 teaspoon white rum (Jamaican 100% proof optional)

In large bowl combine grated coconut, water, evaporated milk, sugar, cinnamon, nutmeg, vanilla, salt, and rum. Mix together then add baking soda, baking powder and flour (one cup at a time); mix well. Then, add melted butter and beaten egg; continue mixing until thick and smooth. Prepare baking pan using Pam, butter or margarine to coat bottom and side of pan. Pour batter into pan ¾ full. Heat oven 350° bake for 40 to 45 minutes or until toothpick inserted comes out clean. Slice and serve.

Bulla

Ingredients:

2¾ cups brown sugar

1¾ tablespoons salt

2 cups water

1 cup margarine (melted)

2 tablespoons grated ginger

2 tablespoons vanilla

7½ cups all-purpose flour

3 tablespoons baking powder

¾ tablespoon baking soda

1 teaspoon nutmeg

1 teaspoon cinnamon

1 cup flour to roll bulla

In a large mixing bowl, combine sugar, water, and ginger, then, add margarine, vanilla, and nutmeg, mix together until the sugar is dissolved. In a medium bowl sift together flour, baking powder, baking soda, and salt. Next, gradually add the dry ingredients to the sugar mixture. Dough must be clammy and heavy. Place the dough on a floured cutting board, then, dust the dough with flour until it is controllable. Roll the dough to a thickness of about ¾ inch and cut into round pieces. Preheat oven at 375°. Next, bake for about 20-25 minutes or until done.

Ripe Banana Fritters

Ingredients:

3 Ripe bananas (crushed)

¼ cup sugar

¼ teaspoon nutmeg

½ teaspoon vanilla

½ teaspoon cinnamon

1 cup flour

Pinch of salt

½ teaspoon baking powder

Oil for frying

Water (as needed)

1 large egg (beaten)

In mixing bowl combine all the ingredients add water to make a semi thick paste. Heat oil in skillet or deep fryer and use a spoon to drop mixture. Use spatula to turn both sides until golden brown. Serve warm.

Rock Cake

Ingredients:

2 cups flour

½ cup butter

¾ cup sugar

5 tablespoons raisins

1 teaspoon baking powder

1 teaspoon vanilla

1 teaspoon nutmeg

1 teaspoon cinnamon

4 tablespoons milk

½ teaspoon salt

¾ cup shredded coconut

In a large mixing bowl sift flour, cinnamon, nutmeg and salt, next, use a wooden spoon to rub butter into flour mixture, until it is fine and grainy (looks like fine bread crumbs) then, add sugar, raisins, baking powder, coconut and vanilla, mix together well. Next, add milk slowly. Use your fingers to work the mixture until dough is formed and a little sticky. Grease a cookie sheet lightly. Shape dough into little rocks and place on cookie sheet, heat oven at 350° and bake for 15-20 minutes or until golden brown.

Cheesecake with Cherry Topping

Ingredients:

3 (8oz) packs cream cheese

(at room temperature)

3¼ cups graham cracker crumbs

¾ cup butter or margarine melted

1 teaspoon vanilla extract

½ teaspoon nutmeg

1 cup granulated sugar

2 tablespoons flour

½ cup evaporated milk

1 (16oz) can cherry filling

Preheat oven 350°. In medium bowl mix 3 cups graham cracker crumbs with melted butter, press on the bottom and side of spring form pan; set aside. In large mixing bowl combine sugar and cream cheese until creamy and smooth. Next, add milk, vanilla, and nutmeg. Then, add flour and mix well. Pour into prepared spring form pan. Bake cake for about 25 minutes or until top is firm. Cool and place on cake plate, decorate with cherry filling.

Plantain Tart

Ingredients:

2 small ripe plantains (puree in blender)

½ cup brown sugar

1 teaspoon cinnamon

Pastry dough (can be bought in grocery store)

½ tablespoon Jamaican white rum

(100% proof, optional)

2 tablespoons Jamaican strawberry syrup

¼ teaspoon vanilla

¼ teaspoon nutmeg

2 tablespoons flour (or enough to make a paste)

Dash of salt

In medium saucepan mix puree plantain with all other ingredients except flour and syrup; boil and stir constantly on low heat. In small bowl mix flour with syrup and add to plantain mixture. Continue stirring until mixture is thick and bubbly; remove from heat and cool. Using cutting board and a sharp knife or pastry knife cut pastry dough into small squares. Use a spoon to pour mixture into the middle of pastry, fold over and use a fork to crimp the edges. Place on greased cookie sheet and bake for about 5 to 10 minutes or until golden brown. Cool and serve.

Caramel Rum Cake

Ingredients:

2½ sticks butter (softened)

2½ cups granulated sugar

5 large eggs

1 teaspoon vanilla extract

2 tablespoons Jamaican white rum
(100% proof)

1 (8oz) sour cream

2⅔ cups all-purpose flour

¼ teaspoon baking powder

1 teaspoon salt

½ teaspoon nutmeg

Heat oven 350° Prepare two 9 inch baking pans with Pam and dust with flour. Mix butter and sugar on medium speed until fluffy, then add eggs. Next, add sour cream, vanilla and nutmeg, mix in dry ingredients. Put even amount in baking pans and smooth the top. Bake for 35 minutes or until toothpick inserted comes out clean. Cool for 5 minutes, remove from pan and place on wire rack, cool for 1 hour.

Caramel Frosting

2 sticks butter softened

1½ cups dark brown sugar

½ cup evaporated milk

1 teaspoon vanilla

4 cups powdered sugar

1 tablespoon Jamaican white rum (100% proof)

In large saucepan melt butter and dark brown sugar. Next, add evaporated milk and cook for 2 minutes over medium heat. Then, add vanilla and rum while stirring.

After 2 minutes remove from heat and immediately add powdered sugar while stirring; mix until smooth. Place cake topside up on serving plate cover top of cake with frosting, then, place the other cake on top. Cover the entire cake with frosting.

Delicious Fruit Cake

Ingredients:

2 cups mixed fruits

1 Pack raisins

1-15oz pack prunes

1 pack currants (optional)

½ cup cherries

1 pound butter

1 pound pack dark brown sugar

4½ cups flour

4 teaspoons baking powder

1 bottle red wine

1 teaspoon lime juice

1 teaspoon nutmeg

2 teaspoons cinnamon

½ teaspoon salt

1-4.8oz Grace browning

1 teaspoon vanilla extract

½ teaspoon almond extract

½ cup evaporated milk

¼ cup Jamaican white rum (100% proof)

¼ cup plain breadcrumbs

8 large eggs

1 teaspoon lime zest

In large covered container or jar put together all fruits, ¾ bottle of wine, and rum let sit for about 4 weeks or more. In large mixing bowl combine butter and sugar beat with electric mixer until creamy, add 4 eggs (one at a time removing the eye), then in a small bowl put 4 eggs white and add the yolks to the mixture; set egg whites a side. In the mixture, add vanilla, nutmeg, cinnamon, lime juice, salt, and lime zest; mix well. Next, add flour (1 cup at a time), baking powder and bread crumbs. Mix together using a wooden spoon. Then, add all the soaked fruits and mix together. Next, add rum, evaporated milk and browning; continue to mix. Beat egg white until a peak is formed. Then, add to mixture; when the wooden spoon stands up without falling consistency is achieved. Prepare baking tins or dish using margarine or Pam generously coat the bottom and sides pour batter into pan two thirds full. Heat oven 375° and place large Pyrex baking dish with water then put the tins with batter in it so that it can be steamed make sure water is always in the dish (this is optional but better results are achieve this way). When the cake raise cover with tin cover or foil paper, bake for 1 hour or until tooth pick inserted in the middle comes out clean. Remove from oven cool and pour red wine on top. Cover, can stay in the tin for several months just pour a little red wine on it when necessary so that it will remain moist.

No Bake Biscuit Cake

Ingredients:

1-8oz dark chocolate, break in small pieces

2 sticks unsalted butter

2 large eggs

½ cup light brown sugar

8oz graham crackers, broken in small pieces

Zest of one orange (about 2 teaspoons)

½ cup almonds

¼ cup raisins, soaked in

2 tablespoons red wine or sherry

½ teaspoon lime juice

Melt chocolate by placing mixing bowl over a saucepan of boiling water. In another bowl melt butter in microwave. In a large bowl, stir together sugar and eggs until well combined. Add melted butter and chocolate. Then, add orange zest, raisins, lime—juice and nuts to chocolate mixture. Gradually fold in graham crackers until evenly distributed throughout the mixture. Line a loaf tin with plastic wrap pour chocolate mixture in loaf tin smooth out evenly. Cover the tin with plastic wrap. Refrigerate overnight or at least 12-14 hours. Cut into slices.

Strawberry Vanilla Brandy Cake

Ingredients:

3 cups all-purpose flour

1 teaspoon baking powder

½ teaspoon salt

¼ cup butter softened

¼ teaspoon baking soda

1¼ cup sugar

⅔ cup milk

1½ teaspoon vanilla

4 large eggs

1 (12oz) jar strawberry jam

2 tablespoons brandy

Mix together Flour, baking powder, baking soda, and salt; set aside. In large mixing bowl combine butter, and sugar mixing on high speed until fluffy and smooth. Then, add flour mixture, milk, vanilla, brandy, eggs and strawberry jam mix on medium speed until smooth; scrape the side of bowl occasionally. Pour batter into prepared bunt pan. Bake at 350° for 20 minutes or until toothpick inserted comes out clean. Remove from oven and place on wire rack. Cool completely.

Carrot Pineapple Cake

Ingredients:

2¼ cups all-purpose flour

1½ cup sugar

2 teaspoons Baking soda

2 teaspoons ground cinnamon

¼ teaspoon nutmeg

½ teaspoon salt

½ teaspoon ground ginger

¾ cup mayonnaise

3 Large eggs

1 8oz can crushed pineapple in juice

2 cups finely shredded carrot

(about 4 medium carrots)

¾ cup chopped pecans

1½ tablespoons Jamaican white rum

(100% proof, optional)

Combine in medium bowl flour, sugar, baking soda, cinnamon, salt, and ginger; set aside. In large mixing bowl combine mayonnaise, eggs and crushed pineapple with juice, add flour to mixture and mix on low speed for 30 seconds. On medium speed mix for 3 minutes, stir in carrots and pecans. Pour batter into prepared baking pan, heat oven 350°. Bake for 28-32 minutes or until toothpick inserted comes out clean. Cool for 10 minutes. Frost cake with cream cheese frosting if desired.

Cream Cheese Frosting

Ingredients:

6 tablespoons butter or margarine

(at room temperature)

1 8oz pack cream cheese (softened)

1 teaspoon vanilla extract

2 tablespoons evaporated milk

4 cups powdered sugar

1 tablespoon Jamaican white rum (100% proof, optional)

In medium mixing bowl add cream cheese, butter, and vanilla; mix until creamy. Gradually add powdered sugar, milk, (1 cup a time) until consistency is spreadable.

Chocolate Caramel Delight Cake

Ingredients:

1 chocolate cake mix (bake as directed)

1 can condensed milk

1 (17oz) bottle caramel topping

1 (8oz) cool whip topping

1 small Butterfinger candy bar

Bake cake as directed. Allow to cool for 5 to 10 minutes. Use a straw to punch holes all over the cake, allow cake to completely cool. Pour condensed milk and caramel topping into the holes. Let the condensed milk and caramel topping, soak into the cake for about 5 minutes. Spread the cool whip over the cake. Crush the candy bar and sprinkle over the cake. Refrigerate for 6 hours and serve.

Banana Split Rum Cake

Ingredients:

2 cups graham cracker crumbs

⅔ cup butter

2 sticks butter

2 large eggs beaten

2 cups powdered sugar

1 teaspoon vanilla

3-4 large ripe bananas (sliced)

1-20oz can crush pineapple

1 tub whip cream

¼ cup chopped nuts for garnish

Cherries (for garnish)

1-16oz can sliced mango (drained)

1 tablespoon Jamaican white rum (100% proof)

Melt ⅔ cup of butter and mix with graham cracker crumbs to form bottom layer of baking pan. Mix 2 sticks butter, powdered sugar, vanilla and eggs to form second layer. Dip sliced bananas in pineapple juice to prevent from turning dark and place on second layer. For 3rd layer spread crushed pineapple. For 4th layer spread cool whip. Place mango or peach slices and cherries in a decorative pattern on top of cake and sprinkle with chopped nuts. Chill to set then serve.

Appleton Rum Cake

Ingredients:

1 pack yellow cake mix

1 package vanilla instant pudding mix

4 large eggs

½ cup cold water

½ cup olive or vegetable oil

½ cup Appleton dark rum

1 cup chopped walnuts (or nut of choice)

Preheat oven 325°. Grease and flour 10 inch tube pan or bunt pan. Sprinkle nuts on the bottom of pan. Mix together cake mix, vanilla instant pudding, eggs, oil, and Appleton rum. Pour batter over nuts. Bake for 1 hour. Cool, place on serving plate, use a fork to prick top of cake all over. Drizzle with glaze, smooth evenly over the top and sides of cake. Let the cake sit for at least 3 hours before serving.

Glaze

Ingredients:

¼ cup butter

¼ cup water

1 cup granulated sugar

¾ cup Appleton dark rum

In small saucepan melt butter over medium heat. Then, add water and sugar; bring to a boil. Stir until sugar is melted and syrup thickened. Next, add Appleton rum. Stir and remove from heat. Pour over cake and serve.

Bacardi Rum Cake

Ingredients:

1 pack yellow cake mix

1 pack instant vanilla pudding mix

½ cup vegetable or olive oil

½ cup evaporated milk

4 large eggs

½ cup Bacardi dark rum

2 teaspoons vanilla extract

1 cup pecan or walnut

Preheat oven 350°. Grease tube pan and dust with flour. Combine cake mix, eggs, and milk, mix on medium speed until smooth. Next, add oil, vanilla, rum, and nuts, mix well. Pour into prepared tube pan and bake for 45minutes or until tooth pick inserted comes out clean. Place on cake plate and use a fork to prick all over the cake. Pour rum syrup over the top of the cake.

Rum Syrup:

Ingredients:

½ cup unsalted butter

¼ cup water

1 cup light brown sugar

½ cup Bacardi dark rum

½ teaspoon vanilla

In medium saucepan combine butter, water, and sugar, bring to a boil, stirring constantly until sugar is dissolve and syrup thickened. Remove from heat and add vanilla and Bacardi rum; mix well and pour the cake. Allow cake to sit for about 1 hour before serving.

Sour Cream Pound Cake

Ingredients:

2 large eggs

2¼ cups sugar

1 cup butter or margarine

3 cups all-purpose flour

½ teaspoon salt

¼ teaspoon baking soda

1 cup sour cream

½ teaspoon lemon extract

½ teaspoon orange extract

½ teaspoon vanilla

Powdered sugar

In large mixing bowl, combine butter or margarine and sugar on medium speed until creamy. Then add flour, salt, and baking soda into creamed mixture, mix in sour cream, then flour, next sour cream then flour mixture. Mix well after each addition. Then, add lemon extract, orange extract, and vanilla; mix until well blended. Pour into prepared tube pan; greased with butter and dust with flour. Bake at 350° for about 80 minutes or until a toothpick inserted comes out clean. Cool cake in pan for 10 minutes, remove from pan and cool completely then sprinkle with powdered sugar, if desired.

Stewed June Plums

Ingredients:

6 large ripe June plums (peeled)

3 cups brown sugar

2 cinnamon sticks

Dash of salt

Water as needed

In a medium size pot ⅔ full of water, June plum, and cinnamon sticks, cook for 15 minutes. Next, remove cinnamon sticks and add sugar and a dash of salt, stir well. Continue cooking for about 20 more minutes, on medium to low heat until it looks like jam and sticky. Remove from heat, cool and place in a jar. It is a delicious desert.

Pineapple Upside-Down Cake

Ingredients:

¼ cup butter or margarine (melted)

⅔ cup dark brown sugar

1 (8oz) can pineapple (drained)

Cherries enough to put in the middle of pineapple slices

1⅓ cup all-purpose flour

¾ cup granulated sugar

⅓ cup shortening

1½ teaspoon baking powder

½ teaspoon salt

1 cup evaporated milk

1 large egg, beaten

1 teaspoon vanilla

½ teaspoon nutmeg

1 teaspoon Jamaican white rum (100% proof, optional)

1 (8oz) tin crushed pineapple

In medium bowl, mix together shortening, granulated sugar, salt, vanilla, and nutmeg until creamy. Then, add flour, baking powder, and milk; mix well. Preheat oven at 350°. In baking pan or Pyrex dish pour melted butter, then spread dark brown sugar evenly, arrange pineapple slices and place 1 cherry in center of each pineapple slice then spread crushed pineapple over it. Next pour batter over pineapple and cherries. Bake for 45-50 minutes or until toothpick inserted comes out clean. Remove from oven and place heatproof serving plate upside down over Pyrex or baking pan, turn plate and pan over. Leave for a few minutes, then remove pan and serve warm if desired.

Banana Nut Bran Muffin

Ingredients:

1½ cup all-purpose flour

½ cup bran

¼ cup sugar

1 tablespoon baking powder

1 cup milk

1 large egg (beaten)

⅓ cup vegetable oil

¾ cup mashed banana

½ cup chopped nuts of choice

¼ teaspoon soda

Preheat oven 400°. Grease muffin tins or use muffin cups. Mix together sugar, flour, bran, baking soda and baking powder in medium bowl create a hold and add milk, egg, oil, banana, and nuts, mix well with a wooden spoon until smooth. Pour into greased muffin tins. Bake for 15 minutes or until toothpick inserted comes out clean. Makes 12 muffins.

Grapefruit with Condensed Milk

Ingredients:

2 large grapefruits (peeled, pegged and pulp removed)

1 tin condensed milk

½ teaspoon nutmeg

Place the grapefruit pulp in a mixing bowl, sprinkle with nutmeg, and add condensed milk. Mix together well. Refrigerate and serve.

Orange Pineapple Upside-Down Cake

Ingredients:

3 tablespoons butter

⅔ cup dark brown sugar

3 oranges (thinly sliced)

Cherries for each slice of orange

2 tablespoons orange juice

1 cup crushed pineapple

½ pound butter

4 large eggs

⅓ cup sour cream

1½ cups all-purpose flour

1½ teaspoons baking powder

1 teaspoon salt

2 teaspoons cinnamon

2 teaspoons ground ginger

½ teaspoon allspice

1 cup light brown sugar

¼ cup molasses

1 teaspoon orange zest

Preheat the oven to 350°. Then, peel and slice the oranges thinly and remove the seeds. Next, cut out a small hole in the middle of each slice. Arrange the sliced orange in the bottom of a 9 inch square Pyrex dish or baking pan. In a small saucepan over medium heat, melt 3 tablespoons butter, add the dark brown sugar and orange juice and stir until the sugar is dissolved. Pour mixture over the orange slices in the baking dish, and let it soak for 20 minutes. Next, place 1 cherry in the middle of each orange slice: and spread the crushed pineapple over it. In a large mixing bowl, combine butter, sugar, orange zest, and eggs, one at a time. Then, add flour, baking powder, salt, cinnamon, ginger, allspice, and nutmeg, mix well. Next add the molasses and sour cream and beat for 2 minutes. Pour the batter over the orange/pineapple into the baking dish and bake for 40-45 minutes or until tooth pick inserted comes out clean. Let the cake sit for 5 minutes, then place the baking dish upside down on a cake plate for about 15 minutes, then remove the baking dish. Serve warm if desired.

Lemon Zing Upside-Down Cake

Ingredients:

¼ cup butter or margarine, melted

⅔ cup dark brown sugar

3 large lemons, peel and sliced into ¼ inch thick

(Make hole in the middle for cherries)

Cherries (enough to put in the middle of each lemon slice)

1⅓ cup all-purpose flour

¾ cup granulated sugar

⅓ cup shortening

1½ teaspoons baking powder

½ teaspoon salt

1 cup evaporated milk

1 large egg (beaten)

1 teaspoon vanilla

½ teaspoon nutmeg

1 teaspoon Jamaican white rum (100% proof, optional)

1 (8oz) tin crushed pineapple

In medium bowl, mix together shortening, granulated sugar, salt, vanilla, and nutmeg until creamy. Next, add flour, baking powder, and milk, mix well. In a small bowl marinate lemon slices in melted butter and dark brown sugar. Arrange lemon slices in baking pan, place 1 cherry in the center of each lemon slice, then, pour the sugar mixture on it. Next, spread crushed pineapple over lemon slices, and cherries. Then, pour batter, preheat oven at 350°. Bake for about 45-50 minutes or until toothpick inserted comes out clean. Remove from oven and place heatproof serving plate upside down over baking pan. Leave for a few minutes, then remove baking pan and serve warm if desired.

Delicious Three Milk Cake

Ingredients:

2 cups sugar

2 cups all-purpose flour

2 teaspoons baking soda

¼ teaspoon salt

6 large eggs

Separate eggs into two bowls. In a medium bowl Wisk the whites until firm then add egg yolks and sugar to egg white mixture continue to mix constantly. Then, add flour, baking soda, salt and milk. Prepare baking pan, with butter and dust with flour. Bake at 350° for 30—40 minutes. Allow to cool then use a straw to punch holes all over the cake.

Filling:

Ingredients:

1 cup sugar

1 tin condensed milk

1 can evaporated milk

1 large egg yolk

½ teaspoon vanilla

¼ teaspoon nutmeg

Mix all ingredients together and pour over the cake, until it is all absorbed.

Topping:

Ingredients:

3 large egg whites

1 cup clear maple syrup

1 cup powdered sugar

½ teaspoon lime juice

1 tablespoon Jamaican white rum

Beat egg whites until firm add maple syrup, lime juice powdered sugar, and white rum beat until smooth. Pour on top of cake and serve.

Chocolate Cake

Ingredients:

1 cup shortening

2 cups light brown sugar

¼ teaspoon salt

1 teaspoon vanilla

½ teaspoon nutmeg

2 large eggs

2½ cups all-purpose flour

1 cup evaporated milk

½ cup cocoa

1½ teaspoons baking soda

½ teaspoon baking powder

1 cup hot water

In a large mixing bowl, combine shortening, sugar, salt, and vanilla, add eggs and beat until creamy. In a small bowl mix together cocoa, baking soda, baking powder and hot water, then, add to creamed mixture. Next, add eggs, flour and nutmeg, mix for 2 minutes, then, add milk and continue mixing until combined. Prepare baking pan with butter and dust with flour. Pour batter in baking pan, preheat oven 350° bake for about 40 minutes or until toothpick inserted comes out clean.

Carrot Cake

Ingredients:

2 cups all-purpose flour

2 cups light brown sugar

1 teaspoon baking powder

1 teaspoon baking soda

¾ teaspoon salt

1 teaspoon cinnamon

¼ teaspoon nutmeg

3 cups finely shredded carrot

1 cup olive oil

4 large eggs (beaten)

Prepare baking pan with butter and dust with flour. In large mixing bowl, combine flour, sugar, baking powder, baking soda, salt, nutmeg and cinnamon. Then, add carrot, oil, and eggs. Mix until moistened for about 2 minutes. Pour into prepared baking pan. Bake at 325° for 45 to 50 minutes or until toothpick inserted comes out clean. Cool, spread with cream cheese frosting, if desired.

Sweet Potato Pie

Ingredients:

2 large sweet potatoes cooked

¼ cup butter or margarine, melted

½ cup granulated sugar

2 large eggs (beaten)

1 teaspoon vanilla extract

½ teaspoon nutmeg

½ teaspoon cinnamon

½ cup milk

⅓ tin condensed milk

1 teaspoon white rum (optional)

9 inch unbaked pie crust

Heat oven 350°. Peel and boil sweet potatoes until cooked. In large mixing bowl place potatoes mash and cool, add melted butter and sugar; mix thoroughly. Add beaten eggs, vanilla, spices, and milk (batter should be smooth). Poor into unbaked pie crust. Bake for 1 hour or until pie crust is golden brown and mixture is firm and cooked.

Tasty Bread Pudding

Ingredients:

1 loaf sliced bread (white or whole wheat)

¼ cup raisins

3-4 cups milk

3 large eggs (beaten)

1 cup granulated sugar or light brown sugar

2 tablespoons vanilla extract

2 teaspoons cinnamon

½ teaspoon nutmeg

3 tablespoons butter or margarine melted

Baking Pyrex dish

1 tablespoon white rum (optional)

In large mixing bowl break bread into small pieces and add milk. Make sure the bread is completely covered with milk then add the raisins, sugar, eggs, vanilla, cinnamon, nutmeg and rum mix well. Cover with plastic wrap and place in refrigerator for at least 30 minutes. Preheat oven at 350°. Pour into ungreased baking dish. Bake for 45-50 minutes or until toothpick inserted in the middle comes out clean.

Jamaican Matrimony

Ingredients:

7 star-apples (very ripe)

5 oranges (peeled, pegged and pulp removed)

¾ can condensed milk

¼ teaspoon nutmeg

Wash the star apples thoroughly, then, cut them in halves. Remove the pulp and the seeds. Next, peel and pegged, the oranges and remove the pulp. Place the star-apple and orange in a medium bowl. Combine star-apple and oranges pulps, then, add condensed milk and nutmeg. Mix together well. Refrigerate and serve.

Egg Custard

Ingredients:

8 large eggs (beaten)

1 can condensed milk

½ cup evaporated milk

1 teaspoon vanilla

½ teaspoon nutmeg

½ teaspoon cinnamon

1 teaspoon lime juice or lemon juice

½ teaspoon lemon zest

1 tablespoon white rum (Jamaican 100% proof, optional)

1 tablespoon granulated sugar

Whip together eggs condensed milk, evaporated milk, vanilla, white rum, nutmeg, cinnamon, lemon zest and lime juice. Pour into small Pyrex bowls or one large Pyrex dish place in container with water in the oven bake at 350° for 10-15 minutes or until bake. Refrigerate and serve.

Stewed Cashew

Ingredients:

6 large ripe cashews (seeds removed)

2 cinnamon sticks

3 cups dark brown sugar

Dash of salt

Water

Squeeze out the juice and thoroughly wash the cashews, place in a medium size pot half full of water with cinnamon sticks. Cook for 15 minutes, then, remove cinnamon sticks. Add sugar and dash of salt, stir well, continue cooking stirring constantly on medium to low heat, until it is sticky and looks like jam. Remove from heat, cool and place in a jar. Serve with Jamaican hard dough bread or bread of choice.

Papaya Jam

Ingredients:

1 medium size ripe papaya (peeled, cut in small chunks)

2 cinnamon sticks

½ teaspoon nutmeg

½ teaspoon ground cinnamon

1 teaspoon vanilla extract

3 cups brown sugar

Dash of salt

Water as needed

In a medium pot ½ full of water, add papaya and cinnamon sticks, cook for 15 minutes. Then, remove the cinnamon sticks. Next, add, sugar, cinnamon, nutmeg, vanilla, and a dash of salt. Continue stirring until the papaya is broken up and the sugar is completely dissolved, and the jam is sticky. Remove from heat, cool and place in a jar.

Coconut Puff (Gizzada)

Pastry

Ingredients:

4 cups of flour

2 teaspoons of salt

6 tablespoons butter/margarine

3 ½ tablespoons shortening

1 cup of cold water

In a large bowl sift the flour and salt together. Cut the butter and shortening into small pieces, add to the flour mixture, add the cold water. Mix together with your fingers until the mixture looks like breadcrumbs. Press the pastry dough in a ball, wrap it in plastic wrap and place it in the refrigerator for 30 minutes. Next, roll the dough in a thin layer, use a coffee mug and cut about 16-18 circles from the dough. Crimp the edges to form a pastry cup. Place the pastry cups on a greased cookie sheet. Preheat oven at 350°, bake for 12 minutes, remove, from oven while preparing the filling.

Filling

Ingredients:

2 large dry coconuts (grated) about 3-4 cups

2 cups of brown sugar

½ teaspoon of grated nutmeg

2 tablespoons water

2 teaspoons butter

1 teaspoon cinnamon

1 teaspoon vanilla

1 teaspoon ground ginger

Dash of salt

Then, grate the coconut, next place coconut in a medium saucepan or aluminum Dutch pot, add sugar, nutmeg, cinnamon, ginger and water. Cook on medium heat, stirring constantly for about 10-15 minutes; add the butter and continue stirring for 5 minutes. Remove from heat and fill the pastry cups generously. If the mixture is getting a little dry add a little water and stir. Bake for about 15 minutes.

Coconut Cookies

Ingredients:

⅓ cup butter, softened

3oz cream cheese (at room temperature)

¼ cup granulated sugar

1 teaspoon almond extract

1 teaspoon rum extract

2 tablespoons orange juice

¼ cup all-purpose flour

2 teaspoon baking powder

¼ teaspoon salt

5 cups shredded coconut

1 large egg yolk

In large mixing bowl combine sugar, butter and cream cheese until creamy add egg yolk, almond extract, rum extract and orange juice mix well. Stir in flour, baking powder and salt, mix well, add 3 cups shredded coconut. Cover and refrigerate for 1 hour or until firm. Shape dough into 1 inch balls roll ball into remaining shredded coconut. Place on ungreased cookie sheet. Preheat oven 350° bake 10-12 minutes or until cookies are golden brown. Remove from oven and cool on wire rack.

Chocolate Chip Whole Wheat Cookies

Ingredients:

2 cups shortening

1½ cup granulated sugar

2 teaspoons baking soda

4½ cups whole wheat flour

2 teaspoon vanilla

1½ cup light brown sugar

4 large eggs

1½ teaspoon salt

4 cups water

2 cups chocolate chips

In large mixing bowl mix shortening and brown sugar, add granulated sugar and eggs. Combine all other ingredients except flour and baking soda mix until smooth, add flour 1 cup at a time and baking soda, add, chocolate chips and mix. Preheat oven at 375° bake on ungreased cookie sheet bake for 8-10 minutes.

Drinks

Fruit Punch

Ingredients:

6 cups Grace strawberry syrup

3 cups orange juice

6 cups pineapple juice

½ cup lime juice

¼ cup lemon juice

8 cups water

Small bottle of cherry with stems

(for garnish)

Slices of orange and pineapple

(for garnish)

In medium punch bowl mix all the ingredients together, serve with crushed ice. Garnish with cherries, orange slices or pineapple slices.

Jamaican Rum Punch

Ingredients:

3 cups Grace strawberry syrup

½ cup granulated sugar

3 cups water

½ cup lime juice

1 cup Jamaican white rum (100% proof)

1 teaspoon bitters

In a large bowl mix together all ingredients. Bottle place in refrigerator and serve with ice.

Limeade

Ingredients:

1 gallon bottle water

1¼ cup lime juice

3 cups light brown sugar

Wedges of lime (for garnish)

In a pitcher mix together all ingredients, refrigerate and serve with ice. Garnish with lime wedges.

Lemon-Limeade

Ingredients:

½ cup lemon juice

½ cup lime juice

1 gallon water

3 cups light brown sugar

Lemon or lime wedges (for garnish)

In a jug or pitcher mix together all ingredients, serve with ice. Garnish with lime wedges.

Melon-Limeade

Ingredients:

4 cups cube seedless water melon

½ cup strawberry syrup

¼ cup lime juice

¼ cup light brown sugar

8 cups water

½ teaspoon nutmeg

Blend watermelon with water, add strawberry syrup, sugar, lime juice, and nutmeg, mix well. Serve with ice.

Guava Drink

Ingredients:

3 cans guava nectar

2 cups sugar

¼ cup lime juice

3 quarts water

In a pitcher, mix together guava nectar, sugar, water and lime juice. Refrigerate and serve with ice.

Mango-Lime Juice

Ingredients:

1 small pack frozen mangoes (at room temperature)

¼ cup lime juice

3 cups light brown sugar

8 cups water

Place frozen mango, lime—juice, sugar, and water in blender, puree until smooth refrigerate and serve with ice.

Champagne Punch

Ingredients:

1 bottle champagne

2 cups mango or peach nectar

2 cups orange juice

2 cups pineapple juice

1 liter bottle 7UP

Mix all ingredients in a punch bowl; serve with crushed ice.

Kool-Aide Punch

Ingredients:

1 envelope cherry Kool-Aide

1 large tin unsweetened pineapple juice

1 liter 7UP

1 cup orange juice

1 (6oz) frozen lemonade

¼ cup lime juice

3 quarts water

Orange and lemon slices for garnish

½ cup sugar

In a large punch bowl mix together all ingredients. Serve with ice. Garnish with orange or lemon slices.

Carrot Juice

Ingredients:

4 medium carrots (scraped, cut in

1 inch pieces)

1 tin condensed milk

½ cup evaporated milk

1 teaspoon vanilla

½ teaspoon nutmeg

¼ teaspoon cinnamon

2 tablespoons Jamaican white rum

1 bottle Guinness stout (optional)

Boil carrots in a medium saucepan ¾ full of water. Boil carrots for 10 minutes, remove from heat and cool. Place carrot and all ingredients in blender, blend for 1 minute. Taste to make sure that it is sweetened to taste. Refrigerate and serve with crushed ice.

Carrot-Beet Juice

Ingredients:

3 large carrots (cut in ¼ inch pieces

1 large beet root (diced)

1 tin condensed milk

½ cup evaporated milk

½ teaspoon nutmeg

½ teaspoon cinnamon

1 teaspoon vanilla extract

Water

Place carrots and beets into blender, ⅔ full of water; blend for two minutes.

Strain in a pitcher. Next, add condensed milk, nutmeg, cinnamon, vanilla and evaporated milk, blend for 1 minute. Refrigerate and serve with ice if desired.

Ole Fashion Oats Drink

Ingredients:

2 cups oats

1 tin condensed milk

½ cup evaporated milk

2 cups egg nog

1 bottle Guinness stout (optional)

2 tablespoons Jamaican white rum
(100% proof)

1 teaspoon vanilla

½ teaspoon nutmeg

1 teaspoon cinnamon

4 fresh mint leaves

Place all ingredients in blender, blend for 2 minute, taste to make sure it is sweetened to taste. Refrigerate and serve cold or with ice.

Soursop Juice

Ingredients:

1 large ripe sour sap (peel and seeded)

1 tin condensed milk

½ cup evaporated milk

1 teaspoon cinnamon

1 teaspoon nutmeg

1 teaspoon vanilla

1 tablespoon Jamaican white rum (100% proof)

Water as needed

In large bowl put peeled and seeded sour sap with water, use fingers to squeeze the juice out of the sour sap. With a large strainer, strain the juice into a jug, pour all ingredients into the jug and sweeten to taste. Refrigerate and serve with ice.

Kiwi-Lemon Drink

Ingredients:

6 ripe kiwi, (peeled)

2 cups light brown sugar

¾ cup lemon juice

2 tablespoons freshly grated ginger

1 gallon water

Blend together kiwi, ginger and 6 cups of water, strain into a pitcher add the rest of water, sugar, and lemon juice. Sweeten to taste. Serve with ice.

Pineapple-Orange Drink

Ingredients:

1 Large tin unsweetened pineapple juice

3 cups orange juice

1½ cups sugar

¼ cup lime juice

2 quarts water

In a pitcher mix all ingredients until sugar is dissolved. Garnish with orange or pineapple slices. Serve with ice.

Jamaican Ginger Beer

Ingredients:

½ pound ginger root (grated)

1 large tin pineapple juice

½ cup orange juice

1½ cup light brown sugar

1 gallon water

¼ cup lime juice

Blend ginger with ½ gallon of water, strain with a very fine strainer into a large jug. Next, add all the other ingredients and the rest of water and sweeten to taste. Serve with ice.

Irish Moss Linseed Drink

Ingredients:

1 small pack Irish moss (can be found in Jamaican grocery stores)

2 tablespoons linseed

1 tin condensed milk

½ cup evaporated milk

1 teaspoon vanilla extract

¼ cup granulated sugar

1 teaspoon nutmeg

1 teaspoon cinnamon

2 tablespoons Jamaican white rum

(100% proof)

1 bottle Guinness stout

First soak Irish moss in a medium size pot ¾ full of water, boil Irish moss and linseed for 30 minutes. Strain into a large bowl, sweeten with condensed milk and sugar add evaporated milk, rum, Guinness stout, vanilla, cinnamon and nutmeg sweeten to taste. Cool refrigerate and serve cold or with ice.

Guinness Stout Drink

Ingredients:

1 tin condensed milk

1 bottle Guinness stout

1 teaspoon nutmeg

½ cup evaporated milk

3 cups water

1 tablespoon Jamaican white rum (100% proof)

Mix together all ingredients, serve with ice.

Cream of Corn Drink

Ingredients:

2 cans cream style corn

1 can condensed milk

1 cup evaporated milk

I teaspoon cinnamon

1 teaspoon vanilla extract

½ teaspoon nutmeg

2 tablespoons Jamaican white rum (100% proof)

1 cup Guinness stout (optional)

4 cups 1% milk

2 tablespoons granulated sugar

Blend cream style corn, 1% milk and evaporated milk. Remove from blender and pour in a large jug. Next, add condensed milk, vanilla, nutmeg, cinnamon, rum, sugar and Guinness stout. Mix well, sweeten to taste.

Sorrell

Ingredients:

1 pack dried sorrel

⅓ pound ginger root (crushed)

4 cups light brown sugar

1 gallon water

12 whole pimentos

½ cup Jamaican white rum

In large pot boil water, crushed ginger and pimentos boil for 10 minutes. Then, add sorrel. Next, cover and let sit for at least 8 hours or overnight. Strain sorrel into a pitcher, sweeten with sugar, add rum stir. Refrigerate and serve with ice. Sorrell may be bought at Jamaican grocery stores.

Red Stripe Drink

Ingredients:

2 bottles red stripe beer

1 tin condensed milk

3 cups water

½ teaspoon nutmeg

Pour beer in a pitcher add water, nutmeg and condensed milk. Sweeten to taste and serve with ice

Tamarind Drink

Ingredients:

1 pack tamarind

2 cups sugar

¼ cup lime juice

6 cups water

Remove the shell and the seeds from the tamarinds place in blender with water and blend for 2 minutes. Strain the juice in a jug and sweeten with sugar, add lime juice and stir until sugar is dissolved. Refrigerate and serve with ice.

Cold Milo Drink

Ingredients:

4 cups of water

¼ cup of Milo

Condensed milk

In a jug pour 4 cups of water, ¼ cup of Milo and condensed milk sweeten to taste. Mix until Milo is dissolved. Serve with ice. Milo can be bought in Jamaican grocery stores or at Walmart.

Homemade Eggnog

Ingredients:

6 egg yolks

1½ tin condensed milk

2 cups evaporated milk

3 cups 2% milk

1 teaspoon cinnamon

1½ teaspoon nutmeg

2 teaspoons vanilla extract

½ teaspoon lime juice

1 bottle Guinness stout (optional)

1 tablespoon Jamaican white rum (100% proof)

In large mixing bowl, use a wire whisk to beat egg yolks and condensed milk.

Next, add evaporated milk, 2% milk, nutmeg, cinnamon, lime juice and vanilla, whisk well. Then add rum and stout mix again. Refrigerate and serve with or without ice.

Papaya Drink

Ingredients:

1 medium ripe papaya

2 cups light brown sugar

¼ cup lime juice

6 cups water

½ teaspoon nutmeg

Peel papaya scrape out the seeds cut in cubes. Place water and cubed papaya in blender; blend for about 2 minutes or until smooth. Pour liquid in a pitcher and sweeten with sugar, add lime juice and nutmeg. If juice is too thick add more water and sweeten to taste. Serve with ice.

Papaya Nectar

Ingredients:

1 medium ripe papaya

1 tin condensed milk

½ cup evaporated milk

1 teaspoon nutmeg

½ teaspoon cinnamon

½ teaspoon vanilla extract

1 tablespoon Appleton Jamaican rum

5 cups water

Peel and cubed papaya, put into blender with water, blend until smooth. Sweeten with condensed milk add evaporated milk, nutmeg, cinnamon, vanilla and rum.

Sweeten to taste. Serve with crushed ice.

Tropical Champagne Punch

Ingredients:

2 cups mango/pineapple juice

2 cups orange juice

2 cups cranberry juice

2 cups guava nectar

1 cup apple juice

1 bottle sparkling wine or champagne

In a large punch bowl combine mango/pineapple juice, orange juice, cranberry juice, guava nectar and sparkling wine or champagne. Stir, together, serve with crushed ice. Garnish with sliced pineapple or lime wedges.

Raspberry Orange Liqueur

Ingredients:

1 bottle Raspberry lemonade

¼ cup coconut rum

1 cup orange liqueur

Pour all ingredients in a large pitcher. Mix well and serve with crushed ice.

Pineapple-Banana Pina Colada Cooler

Ingredients:

½ cup pina colada mix

1 cup pineapple juice

1 small ripe banana

1 tablespoon sugar

1 teaspoon white rum (optional)

Blend all ingredients together and serve with crushed ice.

Orange Raspberry Punch

Ingredients:

2 cups kiwi juice

1 cup orange juice

2 cup raspberry lemonade

2 cups mango/raspberry fruit drink

Sliced orange for garnish

2 tablespoons Appleton Rum (optional)

Mix all ingredients together and serve with crushed ice. Garnish with orange slices.

Lite Colada Punch

Ingredients:

1 cup pina colada mix

3 cups pineapple juice

2 cups orange juice

2 cups mango nectar

2 cups lite Appleton rum (optional)

1 cup peach nectar

2 (10oz) pkg. Frozen raspberries

1 (32oz) bottle of club soda

Blend orange juice and frozen raspberries. Pour into punch bowl and add the rest of ingredients. Mix well serve with ice garnish with pineapple slices.

Tropical Exotic Drink

Ingredients:

1 cup fresh strawberries

1 cup pineapple juice

2 cup mango nectar

¼ cup light brown sugar

2 cups seedless melon (cubes)

2 tablespoons lime juice

1 liter 7UP

Blend together all ingredients except 7 up, pour in punch bowl, then add 7 up and ice. Garnish with pineapple slices, or strawberry.

Fruity Lemonade Slush

Ingredients:

1 tin frozen lemonade

2 cup water

1cup ice cubes

½ cup fresh strawberries

½ cup frozen sliced peach

Place lemonade, water and ice cubes in blender. Blend on high speed until smooth. Add strawberries, and frozen peach; cover, pulse on and off until smooth. Serve immediately, left over may be stored in freezer.

Cold Horlicks Drink

Ingredients:

½ cup Horlicks

1 tin condensed milk

5 cups water

In a pitcher, place ½ cup Horlicks, 1 tin condensed milk, and 5 cups water. Mix well until the Horlicks is dissolved; Add ice and serve. Horlicks can be bought in Jamaican grocery stores or on line.

Tropical Slush Punch

Ingredients:

2 quarts fruit punch

1 pack frozen strawberries

1 small ripe bananas

1 cup orange juice

1 cup pineapple juice

1 liter ginger ale

Ice as needed

Blend strawberries and bananas with fruit punch pour into punch bowl. Blend6 cups of ice with orange juice and add to punch bowl, add pineapple juice and ginger ale. Serve immediately.

Jamaican Egg Punch

Ingredients:

1 tin condensed milk

1 tin evaporated milk

3 large eggs

1 tablespoon lime or lemon juice

1 teaspoon nutmeg

½ teaspoon cinnamon

1 bottle Guinness stout

1 tablespoon Jamaican white rum (100% proof)

1 teaspoon vanilla extract

3 cups water

In a small bowl break eggs and remove the eyes. In a blender blend condensed milk, evaporated milk, eggs, lime juice, nutmeg, cinnamon, vanilla water, and rum. Blend for 3 minutes. Pour into a punch bowl, add Guinness stout, mix to taste and serve with ice.

Teas

Fresh Mint Tea

Ingredients:

3 cups of water

3 sprigs fresh mint

Condensed milk

Sugar

In a small saucepan, boil 3 cups of water, add fresh mint remove from heat, cover and let sit for about 3 minutes. Pour into cups and sweeten with sugar or condensed milk to taste.

Fever Grass Tea (Lemon Grass)

Ingredients:

4 cups water

Fever grass

Sugar

Condensed milk

In small saucepan boil 3 or 4 cups of water add fever grass/lemon grass to boiling water. Boil for about 5 minutes. Pour into cups and sweeten to taste with sugar or condensed milk.

Sage Tea

Ingredients:

3 cups water

1 sprig sage

Condensed milk

Sugar

Boil water in a saucepan add fresh sage, boil for about 5 minutes. Pour into cups and sweeten with sugar or condensed milk to taste.

Ginger Root Tea

Ingredients:

¼ pound ginger

6 – 8 cups water

Sugar

In medium saucepan boil water, add crushed ginger, boil for at least 10 minutes depending on how strong you want it to be. If it is too strong add some hot water. Sweeten with sugar to taste. This tea is good for upset stomach.

Fresh Orange-Ginger Tea

Ingredients

Peel of 3 oranges

6 cups water

2 medium pieces ginger root (crushed)

Sugar to taste

In a medium saucepan boil water, orange peel and crushed ginger for at least 10 minutes. Strain and sweeten with sugar to taste.

Fresh Lemon-Ginger Tea

Ingredients:

2 lemon peels

2 medium pieces ginger root (crushed)

Sugar

5 cups water

In medium saucepan boil lemon peel and crushed ginger for 10 minutes. Pour into cups and sweeten to taste.

Chocolate Tea

Ingredients:

1 Jamaican chocolate (grated)

6 cups water

¼ cup evaporated milk

½ cup condensed milk

¼ teaspoon nutmeg

¼ teaspoon cinnamon

1 cinnamon stick

¼ teaspoon salt

Jamaican chocolate can be bought at Jamaican grocery stores. Grate chocolate place in a medium saucepan with cinnamon stick, and water boil for at least 10 minutes on medium to low heat. Next, add evaporated milk, nutmeg, and cinnamon sweeten with condensed milk to taste.

Hot Milo

Ingredients:

2 teaspoons milo

Hot water

Condensed milk

In a coffee mug place 2 teaspoons of milo pour hot water on it. You may sweeten it with condensed milk to taste or coffee creamer with sweetener or other sugar. Milo may be bought in Jamaican grocery stores or at Walmart stores.

Hot Horlicks

Ingredients:

3 teaspoons Horlicks

Hot water

Condensed milk

In a coffee mug place 3 teaspoons Horlicks, add hot water and sweeten with condensed milk to taste.

Cinnamon Leaf Tea

Ingredients

6 cups water

Cinnamon leaves

Sugar

Condensed milk

In medium sauce pan boil 6 cups of water add about 6 cinnamon leaves boil for about 8 minutes, remove from heat and sweeten with condensed milk or sugar to taste. (Cinnamon leaves are sold in Jamaican grocery stores.)

Fresh Orange Peel Tea

Ingredients:

Peel of 3 oranges

4 cups water

Sugar

In a small saucepan, boil 4 cups of water and orange peel for 5 minutes. Remove from heat, cover for about 3 minutes, then pour into cups and sweeten with sugar to taste. This tea is good for upset stomach.